G-2
Intelligence
for
Patton

G-2
Intelligence for Patton

Brig. Gen. Oscar W. Koch

with Robert G. Hays

Schiffer Military History
Atglen, PA

DEDICATION

To Nan C.K., whose sound interpretations, evaluations, and estimates of the situation through our years together eminently qualify her as my G-2

Book Design by Ian Robertson.
Copyright © 1999 by Robert G. Hays.
Library of Congress Catalog Number: 98-89030

Printed in China
ISBN: 0-7643-0800-9

We are interested in hearing from authors with book ideas on related topics.

Published by Schiffer Publishing Ltd.
4880 Lower Valley Road
Atglen, PA 19310
Phone: (610) 593-1777
FAX: (610) 593-2002
E-mail: Schifferbk@aol.com.
Visit our web site at: www.schifferbooks.com
Please write for a free catalog.
This book may be purchased from the publisher.
Please include $3.95 postage.
Try your bookstore first.

In Europe, Schiffer books are distributed by:
Bushwood Books
6 Marksbury Road
Kew Gardens
Surrey TW9 4JF
England
Phone: 44 (0)181 392-8585
FAX: 44 (0)181 392-9876
E-mail: Bushwd@aol.com.

Try your bookstore first.

Contents

Acknowledgments 6
Preface 7
Prologue: In Time of Peace 14

Chapter 1   Four Thousand Miles to Go 19
Chapter 2   Tunisia 28
Chapter 3   Planning for Sicily 38
Chapter 4   Sicily 52
Chapter 5   Operation Overlord 66
Chapter 6   Opportunity Knocks 76
Chapter 7   The Fog of War 88
Chapter 8   German Prelude to the Bulge 98
Chapter 9   The Fog Lifts 104
Chapter 10   The Winter of German Defeat 114
Chapter 11   What Makes a G-2? 123
Chapter 12   Intelligence in Combat 132
Chapter 13   George Smith Patton, Jr. 145

Epilogue: Command Support 157
Glossary 160
Index 161

ACKNOWLEDGMENTS

Were General Oscar Koch writing this, there would be a long list of individuals to thank. I dare not attempt such a list, for I do not know all of those who made early contributions. I would be greatly remiss, however, in not expressing my own gratitude to Mrs. Nannie Koch; to General George S. Patton III and columnist Robert S. Allen for reading parts of the manuscript; and to A. A. Hoehling of Army Times Publishing Company and Carolyn Wenger of Whitmore Publishing Company, both of whom were helpful in many ways in first getting this book into print. For the present edition, I am grateful for the excellent work of Robert Biondi, senior editor, and Ian C. Robertson of Schiffer Publishing, Ltd. And although they don't know it, Carlo D'Este and a Captain Rogers—I never learned her first name—both were instrumental in persuading me that this book should once again be available. Mr. D'Este, in a personal letter, offered unstinting praise for Oscar Koch's performance as Patton's intelligence officer. Capt. Rogers, in an unexpected phone call from Fort Drum, New York, stressed the need for Koch's work as a "text" for intelligence officers in training. Mary Hays, my wife and trusted advisor, often has reminded me of the value and importance of this book and the need that it remain available.

Most of all, however, I am forever indebted to Brigadier General Oscar W. Koch, United States Army, for allowing me the privilege of working with him on this undertaking and for the enrichment of an association with an individual so rare.

—Robert G. Hays

PREFACE

Oscar Koch has gained in death much of the deserved acclaim denied him during his lifetime, largely through this book. His brilliant record as a combat intelligence officer in World War II was overshadowed by the spectacular successes of his commander, General George S. Patton, Jr. Oscar Koch would have had it no other way. He was a modest man, a good soldier and faithful member of Patton's staff who understood that the role of an intelligence officer was to serve the needs of his chief.

When General Koch's work was first published in 1971, it got relatively little attention. In the anti-war climate of the late 1960s and early 1970s, military history was not the most popular reading topic. In addition, General Koch's story went against the prevailing account of one of World War II's most important battles, the Battle of the Bulge. Contemporary reports and the accounts of historians since the war had insisted that Allied intelligence had failed to detect the massive German Army buildup preceding the Bulge, temporarily jeopardizing the success of the war against Hitler's forces on the European western front. General Koch showed conclusively that this was not true.

The Allied failure preceding the German counteroffensive in the Ardennes, Koch knew, was a failure by higher command—General Dwight Eisenhower and General Omar Bradley—to take advantage of intelligence information readily available. General Patton, on the other hand, had absolute faith in Third Army intelligence reports, which had tracked the German buildup for weeks in advance and accurately predicted the fanatic attack launched by Hitler's forces on December 16, 1944.

Koch agonized over the realization that, the final outcome of the Battle of the Bulge notwithstanding, the desperate situation was saved by the Allied response *after* the German attack and not by preparations made before. He knew, as well, that the success of that response was due largely to the performance of Patton's Third Army—performance stemming from the fact that General Patton did expect the German action and had planned accordingly, despite the failure of higher command to accept the obvious evidence at hand.

Oscar Koch, in his usual precise and thorough way, documented that evidence. He knew his material well; he had been the Third Army G-2—military terminology for intelligence officer—whose work Patton relied on.

General Koch's book was well received by reviewers, both those in the popular, mainstream media and professional soldiers writing for various military journals. At the outset, however, his voice went mostly unheard by military historians.

And early exception was the British historian, H. Essame, whose 1974 biography, *Patton: a Study in Command*, labeled Koch the "spark plug" of Third Army and drew heavily on Koch's work. Patton, Essame wrote, had in his G-2, Koch, "what was probably, in the field of intelligence, the most penetrating brain in the American Army." Essame recognized in Oscar Koch "the most brilliant and original member of Patton's command team." Unlike a great many others who would focus almost exclusively on Koch's role in the weeks preceding the Battle of the Bulge, Essame based his evaluation on Koch's extensive record of service with Patton.

Over time, other military historians began to include Koch among their sources—often as a counterbalance to the traditional "intelligence failure" view of the Battle of the Bulge. By the late 1980s and early 1990s, the record had become a good deal more clear. Koch's work had come to be a standard reference in many comprehensive accounts of World War II in Europe, and particularly those relating to the Bulge. Charles B. MacDonald, in his epic 1985 account of the Battle of the Bulge, *A Time for Trumpets*, reports in detail on the December 9, 1944, briefing in which Koch spelled out to Patton the seriousness with which he viewed the danger of the German buildup. It was at this meeting that General Patton vowed to be ready for "whatever happens."

In his highly readable 1991 account of the U.S. Army role in World War II, *There's a War to be Won*, Geoffrey Perret credits Koch's intelligence work as the basis for Patton's preparedness in advance of the Bulge. Meanwhile, he writes, intelligence chiefs in the higher headquarters "had handsful of dust that they threw in each other's eyes."

Charles M. Province, in his 1992 *Patton's Third Army*, notes that as early as December 9, 1944, the Third Army G-2 Section sent a report to Eisenhower's headquarters indicating the probability of an upcoming German offensive. But, he writes, "the report was ignored." Then, on December 16, "The repeated warnings to SHAFE by Patton's G-2 officer, Colonel Koch, were finally borne out."

It is perhaps in the work of Carlo D'Este, the definitive biographer of General George S. Patton, Jr., that Oscar Koch finally gets virtually full measure of credit due. Like Essame, D'Este includes Koch's contributions over the duration of the war. D'Este's 1995 masterpiece, *Patton: a Genius for War*, makes extensive reference to Oscar Koch. D'Este recognizes that Koch was one of the very small number of men who formed Patton's "inner circle," having been a friend and associate on whom Patton had relied since long before the beginning of the war. D'Este also pays high tribute to the unparalleled excellence of Koch's performance as Third Army G-2. In the period preceding the Battle of the Bulge, D'Este states, "Koch was the only Allied intelligence officer to anticipate trouble and plan how to deal with it. Thus, where other intelligence officers were lulling their commanders with false optimism and wishful thinking that nothing serious was imminent, the Third Army made plans to deal with what no one else believed would occur."

*****

I first met General Oscar Koch more than a decade after he retired from active military life. He had moved to Carbondale, Illinois, the home town of his wife, Nan. I was a public relations writer for Southern Illinois University, and also had begun graduate studies in journalism. He was at work on a civic project on which my services had been "volunteered" by the chancellor to help promote the institution's good relationship with the community.

I knew nothing of Koch's past. But I learned immediately that he was a pleasant fellow to work with, who never failed to express his appreciation for the contributions of others. He always was immaculately groomed and always punctual—the disciplined individual I expected a retired brigadier general to be. He also was mild-mannered and polite and had a wonderful sense of humor. I liked him from the outset. Despite the great difference in our ages, we became good friends. Although my military service consisted of two years as a draftee special orders clerk whose only "action" was in a training regiment at Fort Jackson, South Carolina, and whose highest rank was Specialist Third Class, he was especially pleased to learn that I was a veteran. He was even more pleased when I pointed out that Fort Jackson was a *Third Army* training base.

Only over some period of time did I begin to comprehend the magnitude of Oscar Koch's contributions as a military man. Even though I always referred to him as "the general," I had not thought much about his military career.

Like everyone else, though, I was interested in Koch's connection with General George S. Patton, Jr. I asked if I might write a feature about him for the *St. Louis Post-Dispatch*, based on his recollections of service with Patton. He was not enthusiastic about it. He finally agreed, but somewhat reluctantly. Then I began to learn, for the first time, the true significance of Koch's record. The *Post-Dispatch* ran my long personality profile of General Koch, appropriately, under the title headline, "He Helped Decide to Hold Bastogne."

I had taken photographs to go with the article; the one the general liked best was one in which he stood in front of his fireplace pointing out the "Patton saber" his old commander had given him. He always displayed that sword in a place of honor, mounted above the mantle.

General Koch was pleased with the article. He was pleasantly surprised at the reactions of readers, including several old acquaintances around the country that he had had little or no contact with for several years. I suppose it was my *Post-Dispatch* article that gave him enough confidence in me to feel comfortable about combining efforts on a project that was most dear to his heart: a book on combat intelligence. I had learned of that undertaking some time earlier from a mutual friend, John Allen. Mr. Allen, a man General Koch's age, was a writer and historian of note and a past president of the Illinois State Historical Society. I had known him for a good many years and held him in high regard. I was flattered by his suggestion that the general and I should join forces.

General Koch, Mr. Allen told me, had spent months researching his topic. He already had done a great deal of writing. The general, Mr. Allen said, was the foremost authority on the topic of combat intelligence. He needed editorial help. It was John Allen who first broached the idea of a collaboration to General Koch. The general said it was a great idea.

This was the beginning of one of the most rewarding experiences of my life. Over the next three years, General Koch and I worked together on a book we hoped would prove both authoritative and of popular interest. The general, I soon learned, had been working under two major handicaps: his deep and lasting respect and admiration for General George S. Patton, Jr., and his own modesty. Because of the first, he was reluctant to stress the Patton tie lest he be accused of "using the Old Man's name" to promote his own interests. Because of the second, he had limited the use of personal examples from his own remarkably rich experience.

I argued that the general's work would merely enhance Patton's reputation, and that stressing his own experience would make our book more authentic. The general gave ground, but only a little. I wanted more first-person, active sentences: "I ordered air photos." He wanted less first-person, even at the price of passive writing: "Air photos were ordered." In the final analysis, I always concurred with General Koch's wishes. His entire adult life had been devoted to military service. He had served his country magnificently. This was his book; it would be written the way he wanted it.

Gradually, I came to know a great deal about Oscar Koch. I learned that he had no middle name. "My real name was just Oscar Koch," he told me. "But in the military, you're always asked for a middle initial. I just arbitrarily choose one, and since then I've been Oscar W. Koch."

I learned that he was first sworn into the "Light Horse Squadron" (later Troop A, First Wisconsin Cavalry) on June 18, 1915, as a boy of eighteen. He had served on the Mexican border with General John J. Pershing, was in the vanguard of American troops to arrive in Europe in World War I, and was commissioned a second lieutenant on his twenty-first birthday. He organized and commanded the first federally-recognized National Guard unit in Wisconsin and made important contributions as an instructor in the Army Cavalry School. He first served with Patton at Fort Riley, Kansas, during the peaceful years preceding World War II. With the coming of that conflict, Patton called him into combat.

Koch—a colonel at the time—had served as chief of staff for Task Force Blackstone in the Patton invasion of French Morocco. For the remainder of the war, he was Patton's intelligence chief, or G-2. These Patton commands included the II Corps and I Armored Corps in North Africa, the United States Seventh Army in its conquest of Sicily, and finally the Third Army in operations across Europe. After the war, he organized and directed the Army's first peacetime combat intelligence school. He served as director of intelligence for the high commissioner and commanding general of United States forces in Austria. And in Korea, he was assistant commander and then commander of the historic American combat unit, the 25th Infantry Division. He retired as a brigadier general in 1954.

In retirement, General Koch received a grant from the John Simon Guggenheim Foundation to support his research in military history. He had systematically preserved a vast quantity of material from his own combat intelligence operations during the war in Europe; now he wanted to study the German military archives to see how well the Allied intelligence teams really had done their job. Most of all, he wanted to tell the how's and why's of combat intelligence by detailing the techniques developed and applied by G-2 sections in the Patton commands.

With the prodigious amount of work already done by General Koch, it was apparent that my contribution would be comparatively small. I wanted to help tell his story. I wanted to use both Patton's and Koch's names more freely. He agreed, but he still was a reluctant hero.

At some point during our work, the general received a letter from a filmmaker. He was making a movie about General Patton, he wrote, and "Colonel Koch" would be one of its characters. He included portions of the script where the Koch lines appeared. The general was asked to approve the lines. The filmmaker added a significant stipulation: Should the general choose not to approve the lines for "Colonel Koch," the character's name would be changed in the movie. It was a clear take it or leave it proposition. The script attributed lines to the movie character that would grossly distort General Koch's actual performance as Patton's G-2, as well as his personal relationship with his commander. He declined to approve the script, but offered to help "correct" it. He never heard from the filmmaker again. When the movie, "Patton," appeared, the Koch character had been changed to "Colonel Gaston Bell." It was a minor role played by Lawrence Dobkin, an excellent actor who well could have captured the true Oscar Koch. All the inaccuracies of character and fact in the movie—and there were many—were overshadowed by the superb, Oscar-winning acting of George C. Scott in the role of Patton. The movie was exceptionally good in many aspects. Oscar Koch never saw it.

In late August, 1966, General Koch was stricken with sudden illness. The report was grave: The diagnosis was breast cancer. He faced his condition bravely and in good spirits, but the next several months were punctuated by periods of hospitalization, including surgery and cobalt treatment at the Army's Walter Reed Hospital in Washington, D.C. The general's courage never failed. But he was deeply concerned about our book, insisting that we go on with our work. He did his part from a hospital bed.

General Oscar Koch died May 16, 1970, after having seen our manuscript through to completion. Our final conversation concerned publication. I had lost a dear friend, a friend that I admired and respected immensely. Mrs. Koch asked me to deliver the eulogy at the general's funeral. There was no more fitting person for that duty, she said; she knew the general looked on me much as if I had been their son. I managed to do it. It was one of the most difficult things I ever have done—yet one of those in which I take the most pride.

I devoted as much time and energy as I could spare during the following year to seeing the book through to completion. I regret that General Koch was not able to see the impact of his work on military historians who write today about World War II, or know the way the record of his performance has influenced countless military intelligence officers in the decades since the end of that conflict. I suspect that, if he had, he would brush it off with a modest, "It was a team effort."

—Robert G. Hays
October, 1998

PROLOGUE

Between World Wars I and II, the assignment of a Regular Army officer as an intelligence officer with a troop unit was one of insignificance. Particularly at lower echelons, authorization for an intelligence officer provided a handy slot in which to place one whose varied talents could be utilized in many other ways: as recorder of boards of officers, as defense counsel or trial judge advocate for special or general courts-martial, as post exchange officer, or just about any other assignment imaginable "in addition to other duties." The "other duties" usually meant intelligence.

If classified documents—then only "Secret" or "Confidential" categories—were within the headquarters, chances were excellent that the regimental intelligence officer, S-2, was never aware of their presence, let alone their content. His job was one of requisitioning maps for small unit training and exercises, but little more. If his regiment were part of a brigade or division, the duty was slightly more active—in spurts. Corps or armies were not in existence and problems related to their employment were restricted to the higher military institutions of learning.

There was no declared enemy. Friendly troops opposed one another in simulated battle on military reservations on which they were garrisoned, or in map problems and exercises. Occasionally, by special arrangement, they would be authorized to extend their maneuver areas to nearby private properties during seasons when crops presented no problems and when cattle would not be affected by open gates or temporary gaps in wire fences.

The "reds" and "blues" were always at war—always on American soil, always similarly equipped, always following orthodox American tactical principles and techniques.

As late as January, 1939, there were only four *Training Regulations* relating to the subject of intelligence: "Visual Signaling," "Aerial Photo Mapping," "Scouting and Patrolling," and "Tactical Interpretation of Aerial Photographs." The last of these had been published in April, 1926.

Service regulations pertaining to each branch did contain a smattering of related subjects, applicable to the particular type of command (infantry, cavalry, artillery). Yet the artillery regiment, though greatly concerned with its firing techniques, paid little attention to the techniques of locating enemy targets to shoot at. No intelligence officer was provided for in its table of organization.

There was also in existence a part of a volume of *Basic Field Manuals* entitled "Combat Intelligence." Its twenty-nine paragraphs were included on twenty-four printed pages, about four by six inches in size.

In 1940, the manual on "Combat Intelligence" was more realistically revised. "The Examination of Enemy Personnel, Repatriates, Documents, and Materiel" made its appearance, as did other units covering plans for the distribution of maps, counterintelligence, and identification of friendly aircraft.

By 1941, the intelligence publications had grown in number to fourteen works, and some technical manuals had made their appearance. Only eight more had been added by July, 1942, by which time troops of the United States had already taken to the field in World War II.

So wartime intelligence officers were trained on the job, some at special courses in the service schools, others incidental to their training at their branch schools, and others solely with their troops in the field.

*****

In 1939, authorized enlisted strength of the Regular Army was 165,000 men. Including the Air Corps as it did then, the total number of Regular Army officers authorized was 12,800. Of these, 1,860 were medical and medical administrative officers, veterinarians, chaplains, and professors at the United States Military Academy. There were included sixty-seven general officers—twenty-one major generals, forty-six brigadiers. Only the chief of staff carried a four-star rank.

For officers of the line, there were three general types of duty: with the troops, with the War Department General Staff, or with reserve or National Guard components on the Detached Officers' List (commonly referred to as the DOL). Duty with troops was regarded as the most desirable. Not only was there a certain satisfaction in direct contact with soldiers, but on duty with troops, housing was usually plentiful and reasonably adequate. Then, too, post life provided more "fringe" benefits.

Frequently isolated, Army posts provided the basic necessities for military personnel and their families. The colonel—there were 768 of them on the promotion list of the Army—usually served in the dual capacity of regimental and post commander. He was "King Bee."

As an officer grew in rank and stature, the military education system tended to keep him professionally abreast of the times. As a young and junior officer, once his branch basic course was completed as a resident of his service school, he could look forward to going back to take the advanced course. Then, if qualified, he would continue one day through the Command and General Staff School at Fort Leavenworth and finally, he hoped, the Army War College. Competition was keen. Even among the qualified, selection was based on so many per year per branch, and there was the further restriction of age limits. Time waited for no man.

Leavenworth graduates were eligible for and practically assured a detail with the General Staff Corps, either on the War Department General Staff or on General Staff duty with troops. Graduates of the Army War College had that "something" which set them aside as nominees for general officer rank, either as commanders in the field or as "Gs" of the War Department General Staff in time of war.

In the years in between, some officers would do duty with junior or senior ROTC (Reserve Officer Training Corps) units at high schools, colleges, or universities, others with the Organized Reserves and still others as instructors of the National Guard.

Whatever the assignment, the officer took it in stride. He would check the promotion list from time to time to see where he stood—how many files he had gained through resignations, retirements, or deaths. Three hundred a year, in the lower bracket, was a good average figure. If he were at the bottom of the World War I "hump," he might, at age sixty-four, having completed close to forty years of service (with some fifteen years as a lieutenant), retire as a regimental commander— a colonel. Maybe.

*****

But always, in order of preference, command duty came first, then staff. Details as students at service schools were sought "to get it on the record," and details as instructors at these schools were considered to add to professional prestige. But for some reason, except for some posts in the military attaché system, and except for a limited number of posts in staff capacities, intelligence was at the bottom of the prestige list.

General Omar N. Bradley "scrupulously"* avoided such assignments. General George S. Patton, Jr., on the other hand, was detailed as G-2 of the Hawaiian Department as a cavalry major. Whether it was to his professional liking is unknown. Maybe it served as a means of getting on the then otherwise very limited foreign service roster, or maybe it was a way of doing his tour of staff duty to get it over with. Or he may not have been given much choice in the matter.

But why this desire to avoid intelligence duty?

It may well have reflected the overall War Department, or national, attitude. As provided for in the National Defense Act, the War Department General Staff Gs were major generals. All except G-2, intelligence. G-2 was a colonel. Was this duty—one to become so vital overnight—considered as one with no future? An uninviting professional dead end? One with co-equal staff status and responsibility, but not co-equal stature and rank?

It may have been that the desire to avoid intelligence duty in the between-wars period was because, at most levels of command, important G-2 activities were considered subordinate to G-3 (operations). G-3 was in charge of all training—intelligence included. If an intelligence-minded officer wanted to initiate action to further intelligence efforts, he had to get G-3's approval. And G-3 invariably was his senior.

So, if bound for staff duty, why not go into what appeared to be more important and responsible—and probably more remunerative—assignments in the first place?

An air of mystery usually surrounded the intelligence assignment. Those few who were in it probably couldn't talk; accompanied as they often were by locked doors and inner offices, they were usually seen by appointment only. Certainly it was an unglamorous and publicity-shy arrangement, one wherein identities of individuals were withheld and anonymity spelled success.

Added to all this was the possibility that in those days, in light of our military history, intelligence operations simply didn't seem a great necessity in preparation for combat. Our post-Civil War Indian campaigns were based on what scouts heard, saw, and reported. Patrols would then be sent out. In later years the "point" of the advance guard would act as a feeler. The enemy situation would be "developed." There would be meeting engagements. It didn't matter whether the enemy was superior or inferior in strength. Tactical decisions would be made on the ground, "depending on the situation."

In World War I, American forces had relied heavily on their allies for intelligence information. Our allies had been engaged in combat on foreign soil, in large scale, for some time. They knew more about intelligence, and they passed the infor-

* Omar N. Bradley, A *Soldier's Story* (New York: Henry Holt and Company, 1951), p. 33.

mation on to us. Our requirements were usually based on what these allies needed most to combat the common enemy—manpower and materiel.

So maybe there was a cozy feeling that all was being looked after, that intelligence already was in competent hands—a closely-knit, quiet group wanting no outside interference and certainly no interlopers.

But, no matter what the reasons, one important factor had been overlooked in those years of peace. Intelligence officers are made, not born.

1

FOUR THOUSAND MILES TO GO

The hastily called conference was, as usual, informal. The commander and a few staff officers of his command group stood in a grove on high ground overlooking an invasion beach in southern Sicily, a few miles east of Gela. Below them spread the peaceful Mediterranean, now dotted with the ships of war.

A message had been received from Fifteenth Army Group headquarters. It granted a request, but there was a string attached.

Lieutenant General George S. Patton, Jr., directed a question to his intelligence officer (G-2). "Colonel Koch," he said crisply, "if I attack Agrigento, will I bring on a major engagement?"

"No, Sir," was my immediate response.

Patton turned to Colonel Halley G. Maddox, his operations officer (G-3), with a terse command. "Issue the order."

It was July 16, 1943—D-Day plus six in the Sicilian campaign. The United States Seventh Army's restless Patton, having formed a firm operational base on General Sir Bernard L. Montgomery's British Eighth Army left, had taken all of his objectives according to plan and on schedule. Now he wanted more action—to move, not sit. By moving straight to the north, he could cut Sicily in half. An end run, meanwhile, could be made around the western portion of the island to capture the major port, Palermo. But first, Agrigento would have to be taken. Patton had sought specific authority to launch an attack upon this objective. Now, his request had been granted, *provided such action would not bring on a major engagement.*

The staff conference was typically brief and to the point. A critical command decision was made in a matter of seconds, though all present knew any errors would be measured in terms of lives lost. Patton knew, however, that my quick "No, Sir" represented an accumulation of intelligence information which was a sound basis for such vital tactical moves; like all G-2 prognoses, it climaxed months of cumulative effort.

The gamut of intelligence processes had been run. From higher and lower headquarters, from front-line soldiers, observers, and patrols, from interrogation of prisoners of war and civilians, from aerial reconnaissance, from interpretation of air photos, from captured enemy documents—from countless sources my intelligence section had gleaned bits and pieces of seemingly unrelated information, now fitted together like pieces of a gigantic jigsaw puzzle. Innumerable reports had been analyzed, laboriously recorded, and methodically plotted on situation maps. A clear picture had emerged. Considering time and space and his order of battle, the enemy did not have the capability of staging either a major defense or counterattack at Agrigento. That was my conviction.

The attack was launched; no major engagement ensued. Agrigento was taken on the night of July 16-17. Palermo fell on the twenty-second.

The decision to attack Agrigento was based on Patton's reliance on his staff, which he used to full advantage at all times. He never wanted to be burdened with needless detail, but those of us who made up his operational staff were always near at hand and available, consulted when needed. We knew we belonged to the Patton team and were playing members. And, refreshingly, intelligence was viewed as crucial in the Patton commands and was treated accordingly.

*****

The road to Sicily had been long, beginning back at Fort Bragg, North Carolina, months before. Patton had been nominated at the end of July, 1942, to command the Western Task Force, soon to be readied for "Operation Torch"—the invasion of North Africa. The broad invasion plan was comparatively simple. In addtion to Patton's force, there would be an Eastern Task Force which would land at Algiers, and a Central Task Force which would land in the Oran area, both on the Mediterranean. The Eastern and Central task forces would be mounted in the United Kingdom. Patton's Western Task Force, mounted in the United States, would land on the Atlantic coast.

Patton's force, to total 41,000 troops, would be entirely American, with American sea, ground, and air components. Initial aerial photo reconnaissance would be furnished by the British. Three sub-task forces under Patton would be under the command of Major General Johnathan Anderson, Brigadier General Lucian K.

Truscott, Jr., and Major General Ernest N. Harmon. Rear Admiral Henry Kent Hewitt would command the Western Naval Task Force, also to be known as Task Force Thirty-four, United States Atlantic Fleet.

I was assigned to Harmon's sub-task force, "Blackstone," as chief of staff.

My first contact with Patton had been back in the 1930s at Fort Riley, Kansas. When the 2nd Armored Division was organized in August, 1940, with Patton as its commander, I was assigned to the original division staff.

By the time the United States became embroiled in the war, I had reached the age of forty-five—too old for combat except as a "volunteer."

Patton, who was conducting desert training exercises in North Carolina, invited a group of us to dinner one night. After dinner, he called me out on the porch.

"Koch," he said, "do you want to go to war?"

"Yes, Sir," I told him quickly.

"Well, you're going," he said. There was no doubt about it.

That was the beginning of what would be, for me, service "for the duration" of the war. Except for brief interludes, my service would all be with Patton.

As early as the first week of August, 1942, the choice for the African landing date had been narrowed to November 7 or 8—the first moonless night on the hostile shore after necessary shipping could be readied. On August 24, Patton received his initial directive that Casablanca would be his principal objective.

By the twenty-fourth of September, actual landing sites had been confirmed. Truscott's troops would land at Port Lyautey, Anderson's at Fedala, and Harmon's at Safi. First, however, we would have to endure the sobering, 4,000-mile Atlantic crossing.

For the invasion planners, an extremely tight schedule prevailed from the beginning. The deadline for outline plans acceptable to the Allies was September 5, and detailed plans from subordinate sub-task force commanders were to be completed by October 16. Within a period of six weeks we would have to pinpoint enemy forces, analyze terrain and beaches, study offshore conditions, and evaluate anticipated reactions of the enemy. Detailed objectives would have to be determined for forces landing on hostile shores an ocean away under cover of darkness.

Planning had to meet shipping, then extremely limited. Shipping had to accommodate personnel and materiel designed to complete the tactical situation. Headquarters of the Amphibious Force Atlantic Fleet, commanded by Admiral Hewitt, were moved from the Operating Base at Norfolk, Virginia, to Ocean View, the Navy's amphibious school. There the Navy taught combat loading which, as opposed to convoy loading, meant that every piece of equipment, every man, every vehicle, had to be loaded with the units intact in order of debarkation—the last on to be the first off. Priorities had to be figured in detail, equipment loaded piece by piece in reverse order to the sequence in which it would be needed in landing operations. Balance of the ships had to be maintained, and each ship was slightly different. Thus, even identical landing teams might not be loaded in identical fashion. The Navy schooling went hand-in-hand with combat planning.

Strict security prevailed, with information offered only on a "need-to-know" basis. Rosters kept at the time listed only eight hundred "knowledgeables," those who were briefed on any significant part of the operation prior to the actual touching down on the shores of North Africa. This figure included members of the War, Navy, and State departments and other high government officials in both the United States and allied nations.

*****

Security was not new to the men of the Patton command. If we hadn't appreciated it before, we learned it early in the '40s. The 2nd Armored Division was on maneuvers at Fort Benning, Georgia, in preparation for Louisiana maneuvers to follow. One exercise had just been completed and the next would start, it had been announced, after a two-day bivouacked "rest" period.

Actually, the "rest" periods provided little rest. Instead, the break in maneuvers was used for service and maintenance on vehicles, for doing the laundry, and for other such activities difficult to perform under the strenuous rules of war and the prevailing blackouts, alerts, and "be-ready-to-move" orders.

Patton approached his intelligence officer. "I want to test our signal security," he said. "I want all divisions to receive orders alerting them to be ready to move in two hours. I want the orders sent by radio *without* the code authenticator. I want nothing said about this to anyone, not even the chief of staff."

His great personal interest in this phase of training, Patton stressed, was predicated on an experience of his own. A few years before, also in maneuvers, he had caused his "enemy" to withdraw from in front of him. He had ordered the withdrawal himself by an unchallenged, unauthenticated radio order. He did not, he said emphatically, want anything like that to happen in his command, ever!

The order was transmitted as directed, by radio *without* the code authenticator.

Consternation followed. Some unit commanders complained they couldn't possibly make it; they had already started their vehicle disassemblies and overhauls. The chief of staff was beseiged by calls: What was going on? He knew nothing about it. So far as he was concerned, the two-day rest period stood. It did, since, as Patton later expounded, an order never given could hardly be rescinded or revoked. Out of a dozen recipients, only one unit (the Quartermaster Battalion) had challenged the lack of the authenticator.

The effects were miraculous. In a matter of minutes an entire division—communication personnel, troops, and commanders alike—had learned an impressive lesson in security. It was a lesson we would not forget, at least as long as we served under Patton.

In planning for the North African invasion, there was an ever-present problem of keeping security in balance with expediency. Individuals were told what they had to know to contribute to the solving of problems at hand, but no more. Some of the Army planners had to know earlier than others exactly where the landings were to be made. None of them had to know when. That was the Navy's business—to get them there, at the appointed place at the proper time. Except to those at the highest echelon, the landing date was not known until the force was well at sea.

Security is all-embracing and, like charity, begins at home. For those involved, however, the exercise of security may not always seem charitable.

Only hours before our "Blackstone" invasion force was to sail, two strange officers appeared on the command ship, sealed orders in hand. The orders were clearly marked SECRET.

In what was to prove a bizarre experience for all of us concerned, the junior officer was made a virtual prisoner of the task force command staff. The orders, of which the junior officer had no knowledge, directed that he not be permitted to return ashore or to communicate with anyone ashore. He would accompany the expedition overseas but would not, under any circumstances, be permitted to set foot on foreign soil.

Prior to the assault landing, he would be turned over to Navy custody for return to the States. No explanation was given.

The young officer showed intense interest in his secret assignment. He was chagrined when told that the nature of his mission could not yet be revealed, but thrilled to be part of the invasion force. His chagrin turned to outright dismay when the force approached the African shores and he learned the truth. His was a round trip ticket.

Some time later, more complete information came to light. Through circumstances over which the young officer was believed to have some control, security had been threatened. It happened just before the expedition was to sail; time would not permit an investigation. The suspect—who later was found to be completely innocent—was placed in a situation where he could make no enemy contact and where, unknown to him, he was under constant surveillance. His family, mean-while, had been informed of his prolonged absence on a "highly classified" mission!

*****

Sixty tons of maps went aboard the combat-loaded ships of the Western Task Force just before sailing, to be distributed to all units sometime en route. Included were general coverage maps for all larger headquarters, with maps of the more limited areas necessary for the accomplishment of their respective missions distributed to smaller units. City plans were included in maps issued to assault and service troops scheduled to operate in specific cities or towns. Road maps were issued on the basis of one per officer and one per vehicle. Due to the lack of suitable artillery fire control maps, photomaps of critical coastal areas were provided in limited quantities. Fifty sets of air photos of the landing areas were made for each sub-task force, and terrain relief models had been brought aboard by special highly classified couriers just before sailing.

All of this was later to become accepted by the military as routine, but in these early days of the war it represented a remarkable achievement. The intelligence work had been so detailed that the individual soldier would know exactly where he would be, what he could expect, and where he fit in relationship to the others. Charts of the town plans had been worked out in such detail that units were given the streets they would use and the directions they would take, including foreseeable resistance they should anticipate at each turn.

Thus prepared, Patton's forces, landing at three separate points on the Atlantic shore of French Morocco, struck quickly and with surprise. The First troops went ashore November 8 at Safi, with little opposition. French defenders in Morocco had little desire to fight the Americans. They fought valiantly so long as they were ordered to do so, but resistance soon withered. An armistice was reached on November 11, and French and American troops no longer faced each other as enemies on African soil.

Shortly after the shooting stopped, General Harmon was host at a dinner at which French and American commanders, who only hours earlier had faced each other in combat, sat together and exchanged toasts and pledges of defeating Hitler and Mussolini.

Guests included the French garrison commander of the Moroccan infantry battalion whose forces had sat astride the main highway between Mazagan and Casablanca, defending the Rbia River at Azemmour.

"Had we blown the bridge," the Frenchman said, "you would have been delayed indefinitely."

"Had you blown the bridge," I replied, "we would have thrown a ponton bridge across the river seventeen kilometers upstream. And had the ponton bridge been lost at sea, we would have crossed our tanks over the powerhouse dam another thirteen kilometers farther up the river."

The Frenchman made no comment, but raised his brows questioningly.

"As a matter of fact," I gloated, "at the site selected for the crossing, the Rbia is just short of being 215 feet wide. The approaches and exits are both good. The river should, at this time of the year, be at normal stage. But to meet higher water in the event there had been unseasonable rains, we brought an extra fifteen feet of bridging material along."

The French commander could hardly hide his amazement. Had any of the American officers been to North Africa before? No? Then how did they know all these things'?

The answer was simple; our intelligence had been at work.

In planning the North African invasion, Patton had assigned "Blackstone" the tactical mission of landing at Safi and, once gaining control of that area, securing a crossing over the Rbia to the north so that its light and medium tanks could engage in a land-based attack on Casablanca from the south.

Planning for its mission back at Fort Bragg, "Blackstone" had undertaken intensive intelligence studies. Among other things, we'd requested and received Royal Air Force air photo reconnaissance missions over the Rbia. From the reported enemy dispositions, it was clear that if the French followed the orthodox tactical principles of defense of a river line they could either destroy the bridge or defend it from the far side.

The distance from Safi to Casablanca, by way of the bridge, would be about 150 miles. Tank fuel consumption was a critical factor. All of the gasoline available to complete the mission would be in the convoy; there would be no more. The limited amount carried wouldn't allow enough leeway for using fords we knew existed farther upstream. We determined that an engineer bridge train would be the best solution, and if it should be lost at sea through enemy action we would use the powerhouse dam as an emergency crossing.

So a ponton bridge was placed aboard the already overcrowded, combat-loaded Navy transports. And its sole purpose was to afford a river crossing at a previously selected site in French Morocco, across the Atlantic, 4,000 miles away!

*****

In planning all military operations, intelligence categorically comes first. Commands are organized, task forces are formed, troops are trained, uniforms and equipment are prescribed, transportation requirements are computed, naval and air support are arranged—all on the basis of intelligence. Combat forces are designed in strength and character to meet the enemy as he is known, and to engage him at times, locations, and in situations which, from the intelligence viewpoint, promise to inflict on him the greatest losses at least cost. Exacting detail is involved; once an operation is launched, no matter how far away the objective, the command must be fully equipped to fulfill its tactical mission.

Without intelligence, the commander is blind. Only through the reasoned application of information supplied by intelligence is he able to make sound tactical decisions. Particularly at the high echelons of command, the commander must know everything intelligence can determine about the country in which he is to engage the enemy. He must know its resources, natural and acquired; the details of its political structure; its economy; the attitudes of its people, their ideologies and characteristics; its climate, and its transportation and communications systems. In short, the commander must know that country as well as he does his own—or better.

The smaller the size of the tactical unit which he commands, the greater his necessity for detailed information. But at all echelons, the commander must know the enemy he faces—or is about to face—his characteristics, his strengths and weaknesses, the detailed location of his forces, the various types of armament he possesses, his tactics, and his military capabilities and limitations. He must know the terrain the enemy controls—the hills, the valleys, the roads, the rivers. He must know the weather, what it may bring during daylight and darkness in all seasons of the year. He must know what temperatures to expect, how much sunshine, how much fog—or rain—or moonlight.

The initial success of Patton's Western Task Force reflected the planning and foresight of those at the higher echelons whose peacetime specialties had taken them well beyond the scope of the previously neglected and decadent state of "combat intelligence." Casualties had been held to a minimum, enemy soldiers had been captured en route to their posts. Even so, we learned lessons in that brief operation which could save countless lives among American and Allied troops in the long, hard-fought campaigns ahead. It was obvious to me that commanders and their staffs at all levels needed greater orientation and training in the proper use of intelligence specialists, attached for specific duties. A gigantic step had been taken in that direction, however; an intelligence consciousness was developing.

2

TUNISIA

In early January, 1943, Patton's Western Task Force was redesignated as the I Armored Corps, and the Fifth Army was activated under the command of Lieutenant General Mark W. Clark. There had been, and still was, considerable apprehension over Spain's political position, and considerable effort was put into analyzing the Spanish Moroccan terrain and the Spanish armed forces there. In North Africa, German Field Marshal Erwin Rommel, "the Desert Fox," and his Afrika Korps were stubbornly conceding ground to the Allies in the West. There was a feeling— and hope—on the part of many within Patton's forces that we would be committed against Rommel. Intensive studies were made of the terrain of Tunisia and of German and Italian orders of battle in that area. To forestall deterioration of the intelligence operation in the meantime, we planned and executed special problems.

As the period of relative inactivity for the troops presented the first opportunity for writing home, unit censorship boomed. Strict security still had to be maintained, and voluminous excisions were made until troops could be instructed in detail as to prohibitions in force. They would later be taught through case examples the futility of such devices as personal codes to keep the folks back home informed as to their whereabouts and activities. It would be futile, for example, to write a girl friend, spelling out a location by using a different letter as her middle initial each time. They would be told that such devices had all been tried and were easily discovered, and that, in any case, censorship would be relaxed as soon as the situation permitted so that those things could be written home. Certain matters, they would be told, could not be discussed with them—not because they, as individuals, were not considered trustworthy, but because of the cleverness of others whose loyalties served the enemy. These people, difficult to ferret out, had seeing eyes and hearing ears; they could piece together isolated remarks into complete stories. For this reason, the troops would be told, it was for their own good that they know only what they must and no more.

The importance of keeping information to oneself was well illustrated in his lectures on security by a young doctor serving as intelligence officer in a medical battalion. His medical school professor had used the analogy in lecturing to classes on professional ethics and the doctor-patient relationship.

"You will find sometimes," he quoted his professor, "that the patient should not be given your diagnosis, for many possible reasons."

He stepped to the blackboard and drew a large numeral "1."

"In that case," he continued, "only you will know. Sometimes, on the other hand, you should tell the patient. In that case, two will know." He added another "1" beside the first.

"But then," he continued, adding still another numeral, "if you go home and discuss his case with your wife, will *three* know?"

A pause. "No," he advised, *"one hundred and eleven!"*

The young medical officer always added his apologies to wives—all wives. He had only quoted his professor, he said. I used the story on many an appropriate occasion, and I always followed suit.

The provost marshal also was of particular help in fulfilling security duties. He was charged with the responsibility for furnishing escorts for, and documentation of, prisoners of war and the administration of the prisoner of war detention areas. He controlled civilians at control or check points, whether in tactical areas or along borders or boundaries. He was charged with traffic control and with the holding of questionable individuals pending investigation by the Counter Intelligence Corps (CIC).

His military policemen physically guarded classified installations—headquarters and other points of great security significance. No matter when or where on duty, they sought by watchful eye to detect unusual personalities and suspicious individuals.

After the shooting had stopped in French Morocco, there was an abundance of troops—French colonials, the Foreign Legion, the Sultan's Guards, French national troops, and Americans, all in varied uniform—plus the European and native Arab civilian populations. The Arabs inevitably were clothed in the characteristic *burnous,* the long, robe-like cloak with hood worn over the head to suit the individual, and typical Arab footwear—flat, heelless slippers of natural yellow color, made of camel or goathide.

Reports had persisted that the enemy was landing agents by submarine. The provost marshal was alerted. MPs were maintaining a careful vigil.

Two *burnous*-clad individuals, strolling the street side-by-side one day, were noted by an MP. Ostensibly they were Arabs, with hoods over their heads, their faces only partially visible. But underneath, U.S. Army shoes had replaced the characteristic native slippers. Had some GI done a little illegal bartering? Or were these enemy agents in faulty native disguise? In either case, the MP was interested. He let them pass, then strolled alongside. Anticipating language difficulties, he tapped one on the shoulder. The response was immediate.

"Go 'way, soldier," remonstrated the "native" in pronounced American drawl. "Don't bother me. I's a Ay-rab."

*****

So far as intelligence operations were concerned, it was not a period of quiet. With redesignation, the Western Task Force G-2 Section had been cut down to armored corps authorizations. Its surpluses were absorbed by various new headquarters, including the Fifth Army, and by special missions of liaison with the French. There were many "behind the scenes" activities: the reestablishment of the French forces (which, after the fall of France, had changed the green and red ribbon suspending the medallion of the *Croix de Guerre* to green and black, mourning the loss of its military prestige), the matter of reestablishing rapport with the Sultan of Morocco and with the Vichy representatives (in Patton's sphere of influence this meant notably the general resident at Rabat and the governor of Dakar), and the alert which had to be maintained until the positions of Spain and Spanish Morocco could be clarified through diplomatic channels.

Not such a subtle job was the matter of reestablishing the lines of communication—the roads and railroads—between French Morocco and Tunisia, and the rebuilding of the ports. Such facilities were limited at best, and had long since fallen into a state of questionable service through neglect.

It was essential that organization of the military units of the late Western Task Force be reconstituted without delay. Having made the original landing in combat teams, the organic units were scattered. As events were to prove, the return of armored units to their divisions was to play a vital role in the fight ahead. In late February, by which time follow-up troops had been absorbed into their own units, elements of Rommel's Afrika Korps undertook countermeasures to stop the Allied thrust into Tunisia. The result was the serious, though temporary, defeat of the American II Corps at Kasserine Pass.

General Patton, who had visited the II Corps informally in late December, was now ordered to Tunisia as its commander. The II Corps, of which Patton assumed command on March 6, consisted of the 1st Armored Division, the 1st, 34th, and 9th Infantry divisions, the 13th Field Artillery Brigade, Darby's Rangers, and seven battalions of the 1st Tank Destroyer Group. The Corps, in turn, passed under the direct command of the Eighteenth Army Group, of which British General Sir Harold R. L. G. Alexander had assumed command in February.

Patton had selected as his II Corps staff several of the staff officers, including myself, who had served under him within the Western Task Force. However, he accepted my recommendation (I had been designated new Corps G-2) that Colonel B. A. "Monk" Dickson, the existing G-2, be retained in that key staff position. I continued to work with and under Colonel Dickson, and an additional officer on the G-2 Section "duty" desk proved a welcome staff increase.

All the intelligence instrumentalities known at the time were at work; the work load of a corps intelligence officer was monumental.

The immediate enemy was now the Fifth Panzer Army, its main forces consisting of the 10th, 21st, and 15th Panzer divisions and elements of the Afrika Korps. We would now be able to study the tactics and techniques of the famed German Panzers on the ground, in combat. We soon learned that German tank attacks could be expected at dusk as well as at dawn; star shells and flares would be used to disperse American assemblies. Lure and entrapment by double envelopment was a favorite technique, based on the German anticipation that about two-thirds of the American force would usually be making the assault with the remaining one-third in reserve. We learned that Rommel's tanks would move slowly to avoid dust and noise—so slowly that unless checked carefully they might be judged immobile. In battle they might stop and appear to be hit, only to reopen with rapid and accurate fire once the attacker had shifted to another target.

We learned invaluable intelligence lessons through our liaison with the British. One important British innovation was the "going map," which showed in various colors the weight-carrying capacities of areas of varying terrain. In Tunisia, the terrain often was deceptive. Although roads were scarce, one would think a tank could move anywhere across the vast open spaces. Because the crusty surface layer often hid less stable soil beneath, however, that was not necessarily the case. And the alternate areas of mountain and flat land formed dry runs and bottoms which became veritable lakes when it rained.

Our intelligence staff gained a great deal of valuable information from the radio monitoring service, surveying both friendly and enemy radio. In addition to learning what it could from the enemy, the service also punctuated breaches of friendly radio security. The service later would be provided for in the American armies under the name of SIAM (Signal Intelligence and Monitoring).

Another important element of intelligence operations in Tunisia was the so-called "phantom" service, in which representatives of the higher command (Army Group, in this instance) would actually patrol the front line situations and report their findings directly to the high headquarters. Although later it would be used in a modified form as standard procedure in Patton's highly mobile commands, the operation as initially carried out in Tunisia quickly drew the general's fire. While the reports bypassed all headquarters on their way to the top, they sometimes led to immediate directives from the top to the bypassed commander, based on conditions the "phantom" had reported on.

General Patton insisted that such reports pass through him, or that he at least be kept informed of the nature of the findings of the "phantom" patrols. Those who were actually making the patrols, he felt, might have only a limited view of action then in progress in other areas, or of an overall tactical plan of which they were seeing only a small portion. His objections led to a favorable change in those reporting procedures.

Air reconnaissance was rather limited, since the emphasis had been switched from close-in tactical missions to ones of a longer range strategic nature. We were provided with some air photos, but invariably they were fewer than the number we'd requested.

We had the opportunity, on an enlarged scale, to see the direct application to combat intelligence of such "auxiliary" personnel as interrogators and translators. We quickly came to appreciate such tools as shell reports (giving direction, caliber, timing, and other factors relating to enemy artillery) and captured enemy documents. And we learned, too, the value of reports from observation posts, patrols, and armed reconnaissance missions of the combat units themselves.

Corps and higher headquarters intelligence officers were charged with the responsibility for keeping their next higher headquarters informed of such reports. We passed this information on by way of an intelligence summary, known as the ISUM, sent at stated and prescribed intervals. These summaries were sent twice daily—shortly after daylight and again after dark—as a minimum, sometimes more often. The ISUM was a cryptic message and, although addressed to higher headquarters, was disseminated as a matter of information laterally and to units within the command of origin simultaneously by a multiple distribution system. It was a factual report, usually sent by coded telegraph, and it did not go into an analysis of the information it contained. Other types of intelligence reports would provide our analyses.

Psychological warfare, later to be divorced from the G-2 activity, was also growing rapidly in Tunisia. Whereas the propaganda used in the invasion had been aimed at making friends for the Allies, Tunisian efforts were directed toward taking prisoners. We told German and Italian troops by air-dropped leaflets that their cause was lost. The Germans were retreating along the entire Russian front, we told them. One leaflet told them Field Marshal Friedrich von Paulus had surrendered at Stalingrad and that 91,000 German prisoners had been taken in the ten-day period beginning January 21—along with 750 aircraft, 1,550 tanks, 6,700 cannon, 1,462 mortars, more than 8,000 machine guns, and 90,000 small arms.

The Afrika Korps was showered with leaflets proclaiming that in only ninety days the British had regained 2,400 kilometers of North Africa in their advance from El Alamein. Not only had the Germans failed to take Alexandria, it was pointed out, but they also had lost Tripoli. In the West, powerful, fresh, and superbly-equipped American, British, and French forces were exerting pressure in Tunisia. Why should the Germans, now surrounded, continue to fight? Their families at home, being bombed day and night themselves, had already given up the African forces as lost. Surrendering soldiers could use the leaflets for safe conduct; no harm awaited them, they were told—only good food!

The propaganda leaflets aimed specifically at the Italians generally were less wordy but just as much to the point. They painted a picture of Hitler and Mussolini on a precipice, held only by a lone Italian soldier who, at the same time, was struggling to keep himself from being pulled over the edge with them.

Several things were by this time becoming self-evident about our intelligence operations. If there had been a feeling that intelligence in combat was a matter of crystal-gazing, or that some occult power could be called upon to give the answers, those ideas were dispelled. There was no longer any mystery about it; intelligence took conscientious application and hard work.

The basic principles of the few manuals and other publications on combat intelligence then available were sound: collection, collation, evaluation, interpretation, and dissemination. Practice had shown that initiative and imagination on the part of intelligence personnel were necessary for successful application of the principles taught.

*****

At 4:00 A.M. on March 23, while on duty in Patton's II Corps Headquarters in Tunisia, I received a cryptic report.

"Based on our analysis," the corps signal intelligence service advised, "there are indications that the 10th Panzer Division is moving south." The "our analysis" referred to intercepts of enemy radio traffic.

I looked at the posted G-2 situation map on the wall. The 10th Panzer Division was shown as "unlocated," but it was believed to be in general reserve in the Sfax area. Within minutes, I had notified all major units of the corps that the 10th Panzers were on the move.

Three days earlier, Montgomery's British Eighth Army had outflanked the strong German position on the Mareth Line—originally built by the French to protect Tunisia from bandit raiders based in Libya but now an Axis bastion calculated to keep the British from joining forces with Alexander to the north. Montgomery's flank envelopment now threatened the Germans from the rear. To the north, the II Corps had begun on March 17 an eastward attack toward the sea, and now it jeopardized the enemy's last lines of communication. Gafsa had fallen to the 1st Division, and on March 22 the 1st Armored Division, its vehicles practically bogged down by rain, had slogged through seemingly bottomless seas of mud to take Maknassy.

A third serious threat to the enemy was terrain. To the east was the open Mediterranean, to the west an impassable dry lake bed. Movement was restricted to a limited coastal corridor, with Allied forces not only waiting at its northern exit but also driving in from the landward side and threatening to cut him off in the vicinity of Gabes.

We estimated the enemy forces, now lacking the leadership of the crafty Rommel, who had been recalled to Europe March 9 on sick leave, to consist of six infantry divisions—four Italian and two German—and two German Panzer divisions, all of which now had to be supplied through the critical coastal corridor. They would try to stave off any further Allied advance.

Under these circumstances, we believed that the southward movement of the 10th Panzer Division meant one of two things: an attempt to relieve the pressure from Allied forces at the southern end of the corridor, or an effort to interpose itself directly in the path of Patton's II Corps. In any event, the 10th Panzers were moving at night, under cover of darkness.

My tour had been routine. I had closed out my reports for the twenty-second at midnight. By 4:00 A. M., I had received seven other reports, including Alexander's Eighteenth Army Group situation report for the twenty-second and the intelligence summary of the advanced command post of the First Army (of which the II Corps was the southernmost command).

The French XIX Corps to the north had reported some movement of enemy troops on ridges in its area. II Corps troops patrolling in Hadjeb reported they had taken two suspicious Arabs into custody. The 1st Armored Division reported information from one of its officers who had been captured earlier at Kasserine Pass and had just now returned as an escapee. Two German dive-bombing Stukas were reported to be heading east toward Gafsa.

Then, at 5:58 A. M., things started happening. From the 1st Infantry Division at El Guettar came the message, "Being attacked at Y 3565* by ten tanks and two companies of infantry." At 6:40, "Enemy advanced to Y 3171," and at 7:00, "thirty tanks and vehicles at Y 4555." At 7:10, "PW taken at 0600 from 1st Battalion 7th Panzer Regiment states three tank companies in column followed by more tanks in initial attack;" at 8:55, "fifty tanks and fifty armored cars in area Y3868-Y4268."

Through our identification of prisoners of war, one fact was now clear for us: Elements of the 10th Panzer Division were at El Guettar—in strength.

While all of this was going on, we were receiving a constant flow of reports from other units. Hadjeb was being attacked by a battalion of enemy tanks. Tank destroyers were engaging a strong infantry attack nearby. Area roads were packed with vehicles.

At 9:05 the 1st Infantry Division reported the results of its action. The Battle of El Guettar was over, at least for the time being. Eight or more enemy tanks had been knocked out, those remaining having withdrawn to the southwest. Enemy infantry apparently was infiltrating to the hills north of the Gafsa-Gabes road. There was no indication that the 10th Panzer Division had withdrawn, however, and a glance at the intelligence map showed a grim promise of things to come. In such terrain there were no front "lines," the front indicated instead by widely spread colored symbols showing which side held the predominating terrain features of that rugged and arid Tunisian countryside—which side held the hills and which the valleys.

The 10th Panzer Division had driven a wedge through the hill masses shown on the map. The weight of the attack had reached within a few thousand yards of the 1st Division command post, located in an oasis palm grove settlement, before losing its momentum. Although the wedge no longer existed as a "V," the map continued to show a clearly defined "U" which looked tactically unhealthy for the enemy. There was no doubt that the Panzers had been stopped before reaching their final objective and now hung in a state of suspense.

---

* Map coordinates of the British Grid System were used throughout.

Tactically, *something* would have been done; they were in an untenable position. It appeared certain they would have to attack, either to consolidate their gains for the night or to cover the withdrawal of advanced elements.

"If it's all right with you," I said to Colonel Dickson, with whom I'd been discussing the situation, "I'd like to go down and see it. It's ten o'clock and if I leave now I can make it. Chances are the attack will come before dark, say around four. I'll be back in time for the seven o'clock shift in the morning."

Being off-duty meant I could be away from the duty desk; a break in that exhausting routine gave me time for liaison visits to other headquarters or for making personal reconnaissances. Dickson approved. I was off for El Guettar.

Information continued to pour in. Early in the afternoon, the 1st Infantry Division reported its command post had been divebombed by twelve German JU-87s. More than two hundred enemy tanks had been reported on roads which could not be reached by Allied artillery fire and the division requested air bombardment. With action picking up in the area, Dickson had posted forty-three reports from various sources by noon. By the end of the twenty-four-hour period ending at midnight, one hundred entries had been made in the G-2 journal, including reports on aerial bombings, additional enemy identifications, and the customary and vitally important weather reports and forecasts.

From a security standpoint, one report had particularly disturbed intelligence: the corps' map and authenticator codes might have fallen into enemy hands. Three American soldiers had been captured in an overrun dugout, and the codes had been in their possession. We couldn't know whether they had been able to destroy them before capture. We notified all elements of the command and put the first alternate set into use.

Shortly after 3:00 P.M., an always hoped-for but rarely realized intelligence break came. Another enemy radio message was intercepted. This one ordered renewal of the Panzer attack on El Guettar positions at 4:00 P.M. Immediately alerted, all II Corps troops were readied to receive the attack.

At 3:45, however, another message was intercepted. The H-hour for the attack had been postponed for forty minutes. The artillery, the message explained, was having difficulties. One battery, for some unknown reason, had moved back two kilometers and another couldn't move because it was pinned down by American counterfire.

For me, having chosen to make the six-hour jeep trip from corps headquarters to El Guettar to watch the attack, the scene on arrival was particularly rewarding. German tanks were still smoldering where they had been stopped in the morning's battle, at the tip of the "V" as it had been shown by symbol on the situation map.

The symbols, I now saw, had graphically and accurately forecast the events to come. Not until I arrived at the 1st Infantry Division command post, however, did I learn of the enemy messages which had been intercepted and disseminated during my uneventful ride.

At 4:38, the 1st Infantry Division reported back to corps headquarters: "Tanks forming Y 3265-Y 3468. Three believed Mark VI, Eight Mark III and IV observed." Further reports would have to await the unfolding of the rapidly-approaching action.

The II Corps ISUM, reflecting reports received since noon and addressed to the commanding generals of the First British Army, Eighth Army, Eighteenth Army Group, 9th Division, 34th Division, and Derbyshire Yeomanry, was dispatched at 6:00 P.M. and informed its recipients: ". . . ENEMY ATTACK TOWARD EL GUETTAR IN PROGRESS. . ."

As details on the attack became available in corps headquarters, it was learned that the attack had come as ordered, at the appointed place and at the appointed time—and had been received in ready and open 1st Division arms with devastating and deadly effect.

*****

By mid-April, Patton's operation in Tunisia was completed. In the period since March 15, the II Corps had faced an estimated 37,000 enemy combat troops. Included, either in whole or in part, were some of the crack German and Italian fighting units—the Centauro Division, the Superga Division, the 10th and 21st Panzer divisions, and the 999th Division—as well as portions of an Arab volunteer battalion and a number of miscellaneous groups and task forces. The II Corps command and the responsibility for completion of its task in North Africa were now turned over to Patton's deputy commander, Brigadier General Omar N. Bradley, later to become Patton's commander and to prove one of the Allies' most able field generals.

Patton was returned to command of the I Armored Corps in French Morocco to begin plans for the next step in the long trek to Berlin: Sicily.

3

PLANNING FOR SICILY

As early as January, important decisions had been reached at the Anfa Conference (named after the small suburb of Casablanca), where President Franklin D. Roosevelt and British Prime Minister Winston Churchill had met. An invasion would be launched against Sicily upon conclusion of the operations in Tunisia. A "favorable July moon" would later become the target date, with Alexander in command of the combined Allied ground forces. Patton would command the United States Army forces and Hewitt the United States Navy forces, rejoining the old team from the invasion of French Morocco. Hewitt's Eighth United States Fleet was to begin naval actions as early as March.

Major General Geoffrey Keyes, Patton's Western Task Force deputy commander who had been left behind with the I Armored Corps in French Morocco when Patton was called to Tunisia after the Kasserine Pass debacle, was placed in charge of planning, training, and all-around preparations for the Sicilian invasion. Ready assistance would come from Brigadier General Hobart R. "Hap" Gay, I Armored Corps chief of staff. Intelligence would be my responsibility.

On February 12, planning instructions were received by the I Armored Corps headquarters. On the twenty-third the headquarters was moved from Casablanca to the Chamber of Commerce Building in Rabat. The planning group was codenamed "Force 343" to differentiate it from its normal function of Corps command. The other main Allied invasion force, a British field army under the command of Montgomery, was codenamed "Force 545." Alexander's top planning group had been designated "Force 141," derived from the room number in which planners were based in the AFHQ headquarters in Algiers. The overall operation was to be known as "Husky."

By mid-March my small G-2 planning staff had been set up in the new I Armored Corps headquarters in Rabat. This small group, consisting initially of only three men, was the nucleus of a staff which in a few months would total hundreds of workers, including attached specialist teams. The G-2 Section was the first to detail fulltime personnel to the Husky plan, with full realization that we would have to lay the intelligence foundation upon which all other planning would be built.

We promptly began work on an outline, covering information available on Sicily in loose-leaf form and composed principally of extracts of reports containing vital information on general topography, defenses, and order of battle, as well as generalities on signal communications, transportation, and political and economic interests. We began detailed planning on April 1.

Meanwhile, it had been my responsibility to "secure" the headquarters and its ever-growing files of highly classified military secrets. A principle had been established and necessary instructions issued that the number of individuals informed of the plans would be kept to an absolute minimum. As the number of troops, ships, and aircraft involved expanded, so did the number of planners who were informed of vital information—but always on a "need-to-know" basis only. The more critical the item, the fewer were those who knew the details. The system that was devised and used for the classification of the planning staff was comparatively simple, yet it proved extremely effective.

Each officer detailed as a planner for the operation was designated and formally listed either as an "XO" or a "YO." The former designation included those whose duties required complete and detailed information on the entire plan. They would have access to all planning data and maps kept in the tightly secured rooms. The "YOs" would know that a plan was in the making and would be given the data they required for their individual duties. But we would not give them full details, such as the date (when it became known), full details of the forces involved, or the tactical methods employed. And they were denied general access to certain planning rooms.

Before contacting others, planners in either of these two categories would be required to check names against our list to determine who was classified, and to what degree. And the list itself was classified to prevent dissemination of the names. Before talking to one another, each officer would challenge the one questioned by asking if he were on a list and, if so, which one. As the planning progressed, most "YOs" would, by necessity, become "XOs." Although only the officers were so

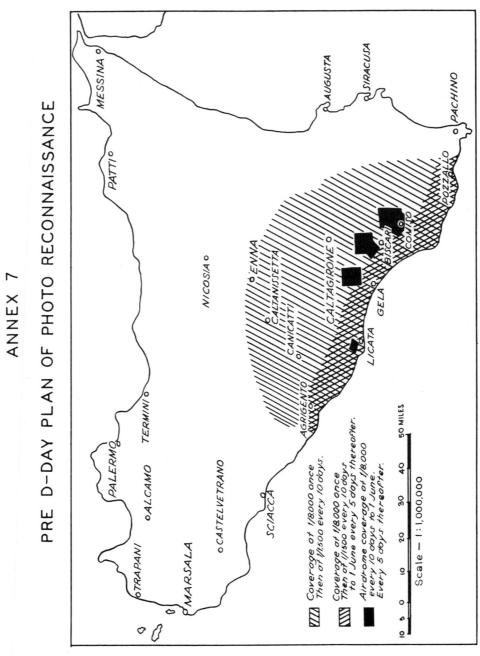

U.S. Seventh Army air photo reconnaissance plan preceding the invasion of Sicily. (*U.S. Seventh Army Report of Operations*, "The Seventh Army in Sicily," October 1943)

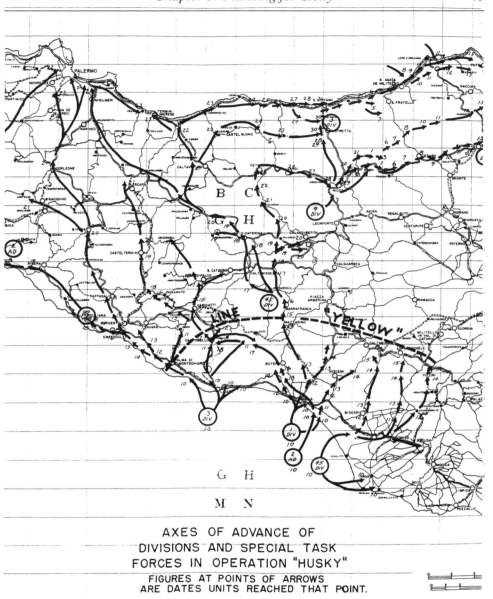

AXES OF ADVANCE OF
DIVISIONS AND SPECIAL TASK
FORCES IN OPERATION "HUSKY"
FIGURES AT POINTS OF ARROWS
ARE DATES UNITS REACHED THAT POINT.

U.S. Seventh Army pre-invasion planning map, Operation Husky. (*U.S. Seventh Army Report of Operations*, "The Seventh Army in Sicily," October 1943)

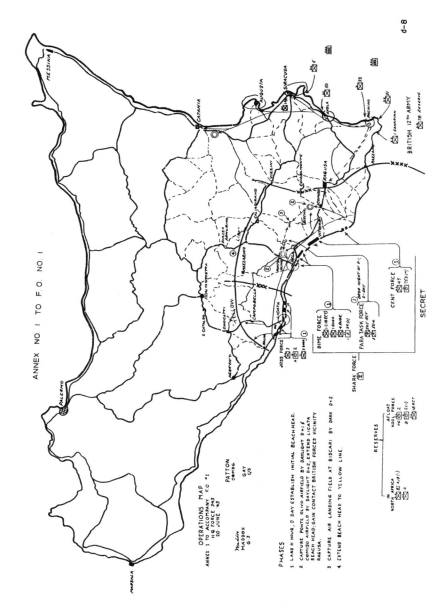

U.S. Seventh Army phased landing plan, invasion of Sicily. (*U.S. Seventh Army Report of Operations*, "The Seventh Army in Sicily," October 1943)

classified, enlisted typists and clerks were designated within the sections to handle planning papers and they, in turn, could deal only with the officers to whom they were assigned and only in a place designated by the section chief.

The provost marshal was responsible for outside physical security, which he accomplished either by use of Military Police or by arranging for troops through regular staff channels if whole buildings or larger areas were involved. The MPs were always posted as guards at the inner gates or doors. We kept all maps covered when they were not in use and we located them so that they could not be viewed through windows.

When maps were requested, the request was made in such broad terms that it covered other nearby places as well. Whenever a map of Sicily was shown, maps of Corsica and Sardinia would be shown too. As planning progressed, each detail involving Sicily was followed exactly for Corsica and Sardinia as well. We carefully recorded the planning maps issued, and we used code names for frequently-mentioned areas.

The buildup of our G-2 Section was made as fast as the availability of personnel would permit. We considered several basic points in planning for expansion of the section. A mobile, fast-moving headquarters would be necessary, based on the premise that what would be effective in a fluid situation would work in a static one, but that the reverse was not necessarily true. A small mobile group to be with the commanding general would have to be equipped to keep information on the tactical situation current so that decisions could be made quickly. More routine duties would have to be handled by those within reach but not in the immediate area.

In March, preliminary invasion plans were discussed by members of the higher headquarters staffs, and on the twenty-fifth an outline plan was issued. It called for a British assault on southeastern Sicily and two split American assaults, one on the southern west-central coast and one in the northwestern coastal area. The southwestern attack was to come two days after the British assault, when it was hoped the enemy reinforcements would be caught en route to their combat destinations.

By April 22, our G-2 Section, now three weeks old, was still trying to get personnel. Meanwhile, the compilation of data and dissemination of information went on; we'd published our first "outline" plan two days earlier. The plan told the subordinate task force staffs what was expected of them in the intelligence field and what they in turn could expect from us. We would publish the formal information later in its orthodox form as an addition to the field order upon which the operation would be based.

The outline plan as we issued it contained twenty-four items of primary intelligence interest, covering the summary of the enemy situation and showing what supplementary information was then available in the form of printed works and studies.

The Air Warning Service would be provided by the Air Corps, and the results would be transmitted directly to the interested agencies. A counterintelligence plan provided for a preliminary "cover" plan as well as appropriate countersubversive and countersabotage operations. We provided false dates and destinations, although recipients were never given a false date or destination without being given the actual ones, too. We would base our administrative preparations as far as possible on the false information.

Plans called for Office of Strategic Services (OSS) agents, operating under higher headquarters only, to interrupt rail and road facilities in the south of Italy and northeastern part of Sicily to deny the easy exit of enemy forces once the invasion had taken place and we had applied pressure. The OSS was still a fledgling organization, relatively unknown and untried so far as Husky planners were concerned.

Each division would issue security measures similar to the "YO" and "XO" system employed at the high headquarters. Intelligence training was to be continuous, stressing enemy tactics and order of battle organization as well as an understanding of British intelligence practices, which differed from those standard to us.

Air photo reconnaissance would be furnished by an Air Corps squadron based in North Africa. We requested photo recon of the entire western part of the island. Invasion landing areas were to be photographed from the coast to an inland depth of five miles monthly until June 1, and then at ten-day intervals.

We especially watched for any changes which might indicate that enemy intelligence was aware of our invasion plans. Railroads and bridges were watched for signs of construction, and we kept an eye on important towns in the western part of the island, checking their configurations against existing town plans.

An important innovation in the planning for Sicily involved our use of relief terrain models. Photographs of the models were taken from a perspective equivalent to sea level and one-half to one mile out. The result was a highly accurate visualization of the coastline silhouette of planned landing areas to be used by units going in over the beaches. By manipulating the lighting conditions under which the photos were made, we could simulate any time of day.

*****

On April 23, at planning headquarters in Rabat, Patton outlined the general plan for Operation Husky as it was then conceived. It was assumed that operations against Sicily would not begin until at least sixty days after the termination of the Tunisian campaign.

My intelligence unit's initial estimate regarding Sicily showed a garrison of 153,000 Italian troops on the island. The fixed defenses were formidable, consisting of emplacements and machine gun nests at vulnerable spots. We had received no reports of beach mines or underwater obstacles, but the island's ports and airfields appeared strongly fortified. Certainly, we thought, enemy defense plans would call for obstacles, defended road blocks, and mines. We found that about 78,000 troops were distributed in three main concentrations on the island, located in the western, central, and northeastern areas. Another 75,000 made up the coastal defense organization of eighty-four infantry battalions and various artillery and machine gun units. We also estimated that there were two battalions of about fifty old French tanks each and a battalion of the same number of light Italian tanks. None of the mobile troops had seen combat, and we expected them to show the effects of prolonged garrison life. There were apparently few first-line troops in the Messina area in the northeastern part of the island. Information we had recently received suggested that principal components of the 4th (Livorno) Division had recently left their garrison, normally in the vicinity of Rome, and were now in Sicily.

The terrain of the mountainous island would have a great effect on military operations there. The Sicilian interior, we noted, was extremely rugged. Mount Etna, in the east central part, rose to an elevation of more than 10,000 feet. Just to the south was the Catania Plain, with narrow and limited coastal plains cut by gorges fringing the mountains on the south and west. The coastal mountain ranges generally lay perpendicular to the sea.

The island's limited roads, full of defiles, followed the configuration of the ground. A maze of serpentines in the mountains, they were relatively straight along the coastline, where they gently skirted the foothills. Inland, the huddled, centuries-old towns and villages perched on the tops of the mountains. Fields and vineyards covered the slopes and valleys. Built during the Middle Ages, the towns and villages were situated so as to make a cross-country attack difficult.

We knew that, because of this configuration, troops moving along the interior roads would not be able to bypass the towns. Every village, reached only after a tortuous uphill grind, would have to be entered and passed through. An example was Caltanissetta, a centrally-located communications hub which would be an important military objective. It was served by three first-class highways, two secondary roads, and a railroad. Yet its approach was a difficult route, at an elevation of more than 2,000 feet, and it was a bottleneck through which all routes led. We could not bypass it.

Although we estimated that the enemy would be capable of reinforcing the island with as many as four divisions from Italy, we considered such a move improbable because of the difficulties of the terrain. And, in the early planning days before the fall of Tunisia, possible wholesale withdrawal of enemy troops from Africa to Sicily had to be considered. We believed that the enemy might reinforce the island with at least two Italian divisions and some smaller German units, in all the equivalent of only a single division in number of troops. There would be few, if any, vehicles.

On April 29, the classified Force 343 planning group (which still did not include the entire I Armored Corps headquarters) moved from Rabat to Mostaganem, Algeria. The movement was made by heavily-guarded convoy. All of our plans, maps and overlays, and still "Top Secret" materials were moved into a tightly-secured headquarters which had been arranged well in advance. A joint planning room had been established in the College Communal in Mostaganem. Meanwhile, the rear echelons were located in Oran, and the inherent security problems we faced were tremendous.

The 343 tactical force now was split into widely-separated groups; some of the invasion troops were to sail from the States, some from points all along the north coast of Africa—the points extending along a distance of well over 1,000 miles. Cooperating naval forces were headquartered in the Algiers area, as was the higher headquarters, 141.

As the Tunisian campaign was concluded and full attention turned to planning for Sicily, top-level Allied planners decided that dispersion of forces such as was envisioned in the original invasion plan was unsuitable. On May 3, Task Force 343 was ordered to abandon the plan we had been given previously.

Instead, a new plan was issued which called for a cohesive invasion effort with a joint attack to be launched by British and American forces in contiguous zones. All of the attack would be launched against the southeastern beaches where a base for further operations would be formed. Force 343's main responsibility now became the south and central part of the island instead of the north and southwestern areas.

This change in plans meant, of course, that we would have to provide an entirely new set of terrain studies and estimates. *G-2 Estimate No. 2*, reflecting these changes, was published and distributed on May 5 just two days after the change was announced. Task Force 343 would now make the assault as a unit, hitting the beach in one area at one time. Although it was too early for us to determine what reinforcements the enemy would make prior to the day of the assault, it would now be considerably simpler to compute the enemy's capabilities as far as time and space were concerned. The invasion would now be a concerted effort on the part of the American troops, and the opposition could be evaluated in terms of a concerted defense as well—instead of an assumed reaction to piecemeal assaults spread around the perimeter of the island.

In the new estimate, we assumed that the British and American assaults would be made simultaneously, that the order of battle previously established was in effect, that no additional enemy troops would act as reinforcements, that the Italian division forecast as a probable reinforcement from the Rome area was actually on the island, and that all enemy troops would be alerted.

We estimated that American troops, at the time they hit the beaches, would face some 15,500 enemy troops, armed with 708 machine guns, 129 mortars, 110 anti-aircraft guns, and some light artillery. Within eight hours, the enemy would be able to reinforce its positions with an additional 34,100 troops, 729 more machine guns, another 258 mortars, and an additional 135 anti-aircraft guns. Of critical importance was the fact that an additional 195 enemy artillery pieces, ranging in size up to 149-millimeter, could also be brought into action in this first eight hours. We estimated that the enemy could have still another 14,200 troops ready for combat within a day.

The target area for Force 343 would be a crescent-shaped coastal plain, fifteen to twenty miles deep, bounded by predominating ridges and including about forty-five miles of actual shoreline. In that early planning estimate, it was necessary to consider the enemy capabilities as a whole because of the restricted area in which the assault would take place. Of four possible enemy reactions to the invasion assault, we saw as most likely defense at the water's edge with a counterattack from the northwest. The intelligence estimate explained our reasoning:

"Capability No. 4 is selected for adoption because the port and four airfields are of the utmost strategic importance and can only be defended satisfactorily at the water's edge.

"The counterattack from the northwest is logical because of the concentration of the mobile Army and Corps troops in the vicinity of Caltanissetta.

"Terrain lends itself to counterattack from the northwest and the rivers would not form a serious obstacle at this time of year because they are reported dry."

A month later, on June 9, the last formal pre-invasion estimate was published and disseminated. Many intelligence matters had been clarified. We found that certain changes had taken place in the enemy order of battle. With the collapse of the Axis strongholds in North Africa, we estimated that the enemy could support a total of eight or nine divisions on Sicily. Seven Italian divisions might be located in principal geographical areas. One German division was believed to be disposed in reserve in the central portion of the island, and a second we believed to be broken into special combat groups. Included were one or two German, and possibly one Italian, tank battalions.

Enemy air strength we estimated at eight hundred combat-type aircraft, of which 490 would be serviceable, and some 175 others (reconnaissance planes, obsolescent types of dive bombers, etc.), of which ninety-two would be serviceable. Until Allied fighter aircraft could be based on the island the enemy air force would have every strategic advantage. All of the enemy airfields on the island were within 120 miles of the southern landing beaches, while Allied planes were based across the Mediterranean in North Africa. Enemy bombers we believed would be based 300 to 325 miles away, out of the range of Allied fighters.

Knowing the locations of coastal installations and ports, backed as they were by fighter fields, we still believed the enemy would choose to concentrate his defense at or close to the beaches.

An immediate and practical concern of the invasion planners was the number of enemy prisoners which could be anticipated. Not only would such losses have an effect on the enemy's tactical capabilities, but prisoners would have to be housed, fed, clothed, guarded, and transported. The wounded would require hospitalization; the dead would have to be buried. There would have to be suitable enclosures, and handling of prisoners would mean additional record-keeping and administrative problems.

During combat, the prisoner count was relatively simple. It was totaled every day by the captors. As prisoners were processed in PW enclosures, an actual "nose count" would be made. But planning estimates made *in advance* involved many factors—both knowns and unknowns. The type of troops to be encountered, for example, was a basic consideration. Coast defense troops being relatively immobile, prisoners taken in beach landings should, in high percentage, be captured in the area of the assault. Available enemy reserves, if the attack to establish a beachhead were pressed with speed, should contribute a fair share. If the enemy withdrew, the number should be less—unless the withdrawal turned into a rout. Later, in more stable combat situations, the numbers captured should drop materially. In any case, we had to have knowledge, which only intelligence could provide, of the number and types of enemy troops present in the area. All estimates hinged on that.

Considering the known distribution of enemy forces, the types of troops and their estimated combat efficiencies, and playing these factors against the Allied operational plans for the invasion, we worked out an estimate for planning purposes. We figured that an average of 2,500 prisoners a day should be taken for the first five days, increasing to an average of 8,000 a day for the next ten days. Thereafter, the numbers would depend entirely on the tactical situation. But for planning purposes, a figure of 850 to 1,000 prisoners a day seemed justified.

July 10 had been established as D-Day. To avoid leaks and deny even casual observers the accidental opportunity of gaining knowledge of the date, frequent loading rehearsals for amphibious operations had been held as often as possible. One day the "rehearsal" would be the real thing. Everything would be done just as it had been done before, but this time for the record. Even then, individual troops had no factual knowledge of either the invasion date or the destination. Every precaution was taken to maintain the utmost secrecy.

Obviously, maps and other classified materials to be distributed to the troops once the actual invasion was underway were not handed out during the rehearsals. They were packaged and placed aboard the ships, however, with strictest security measures in force and with specific instructions issued as to the earliest date they could be opened. Among these materials were handbooks for the edification of the troops. These handbooks, which became routine in World War II, usually included a brief pre-war history of the country of destination, something of its customs, and advice on how the soldiers were to conduct themselves with the populace. A few of the most common words and phrases of the foreign tongue with phonetic pronunciations were also listed.

It wasn't until after all of the security instructions and calendar dates for opening the secret bundles aboard Sicily-bound ships had been issued that we discovered a serious staff error. Instead of calendar dates, the time when the bundles were to be opened should have been dictated by a specific occurrence—"eight hours after final embarkation," for example.

The error led to a serious security problem.

For some reason, one of the combat-loaded ships docked at Algiers was delayed in sailing. Instead of being in a rendezvous area out of the harbor and well at sea as scheduled on that particular date, it was still tied up alongside the command ship *Monrovia.*

On the authorized date, following orders, the commander of troops on the ship had opened and distributed the contents of the packages of secret material. Some of these would, for the first time, disclose the actual assault objective to the troops.

Invasion-ready soldiers, lounging on the deck and comfortably basking in the July sun, were leisurely reading the handbook included in their pre-landing materials. On the white paper cover the title, vividly superimposed over an inescapable black outline of the target island, told the story: *This is Sicily.*

The French harbor pilot who would take the ship out of port and then be dropped and returned to the dock already was aboard. Had he seen the books? Who was he?

Where did his loyalties lie? Certainly this was a security problem, an unintentional yet very serious breach, calling for immediate action. The invasion convoy was under steam, leaving within the hour. Something had to be done.

After a series of brief conferences with counterintelligence experts, we made our decision. Nothing would be said to the troops. We felt an explanation would compound the injury. The pilot and those accompanying him would pursue their normal duties. Nothing would be said to them about the matter either. They would take the ship out of port, and the pilot's boat would pick them up as usual. But when they got back to the Algiers dock, they would all be detained by counterintelligence personnel and held incommunicado until *after* the landing in Sicily four days later.

The harbor pilot and his crew, we learned later, offered no serious objection to their involuntary detention. They understood, sympathetically, that this was war, acquiescing with the typical French shrug of the shoulders and a *"C'est la guerre."*

*****

Shortly before the Sicilian invasion got underway, several officers from the States reported to Force 343 headquarters. Some were assigned for permanent duty with the command, some were on temporary status to get combat operational experience in preparation for their own units' being ordered overseas. Others were War Department observers who were there as personal representatives for the chief of staff. Among the latter was Brigadier General Albert Wedemeyer, then on the War Department general staff.

Newcomers in Patton's headquarters, irrespective of status, were always thoroughly briefed. This group was interested primarily in intelligence, particularly the G-2 estimate. Their briefing, conducted in a G-2 Section room complete with maps and charts to provide graphic support, concluded with a detailed discussion of the enemy's capabilities. Defense at the water's edge was still expected.

When the others left, General Wedemeyer remained.

"It may interest you to know," he told me, "that you are alone in your estimate. The War Department doesn't agree. AFHQ doesn't agree. Other headquarters do not agree. And I don't agree."

According to the thinking of all of those groups, he said, the enemy would initially contain the American forces by defending inland, meanwhile moving its forces to the east to stage a major counterattack against the British. This would deny the Allied forces the vital Catania Plain with its airfields, and, indirectly, the important eastern road to Messina.

Startling, but not new.

I expressed the hope that I was wrong. The enemy's *not* defending at the water's edge would be most favorable to Force 343's operations. Nevertheless, I told him, the estimates presented were based on enemy capabilities as seen by my G-2 Section staff and by me; regardless of what others thought, they would stand.

General Wedemeyer left the room remarking courteously and in good spirit, "Well, you're wrong. Wait and see."

With the invasion force ready for launching, I wouldn't have long to wait. The course of events in the immediate future could have a far-reaching influence on the direction of the war in Europe. Time—and the enemy—would provide the answer soon enough.

4

SICILY

"A rare summer windstorm kicked the Mediterranean into a white-capped frenzy the morning of 9 July 1943. Now wallowing in the troughs of twenty- to thirty-foot seas, now turning and plunging their noses into green water and shaking spray off their structures, the ships of history's greatest armada converged toward Malta. Battleships and monitors, cruisers, destroyers, and escort vessels shepherded their flock of transports and invasion ships across the heaving sea. Occasionally a flight of bombers swept overhead against the storm, intent on their mission of softening enemy defenses before the invasion."

So reads the United States Seventh Army's *Report of Operations* on the African-based invasion of Sicily. The hour of reckoning had come. The test of our pre-invasion intelligence calculations would begin as soon as the initial wave of Allied troops hit the Sicilian beaches. Once again, errors would be measured in terms of lives lost—a sobering thought to all of us in the G-2 Section.

Of most immediate concern to us, however, was the weather, a concern accented by the operation report:

"More than seasickness was caused by that storm. In the command posts above decks there was consternation. The whole delicately timed plan, culminating in the moment for which the whole world was waiting, hung subject to the caprices of nature. What if the sea were too high for the small boats to land? What if the high wind scattered the troop carriers of the airborne assault? Plans were made to delay the invasion one day.

"But by late afternoon, as Malta appeared abeam and then dropped astern, with the Sicilian coast only ninety miles away, the wind seemed to slacken and the sea level off. The decision was made to carry on as planned. The gray ships that covered hundreds of square miles of ocean maintained their northward course. And far behind them, at Kairouan in Tunisia, the fleet of C-47 transports received orders to warm up and take aboard their cargo of parachutists (of the 82nd Airborne Division). A few hours later, the air fleet roared over Malta to strike the first blow of the long-planned assault."

Unfortunately, that planned "first blow" was destined to be the first one to miss the target. A forty-mile headwind was still blowing as the parachute task force searched southern Sicily for its drop zone—the high ground north and east of Ponte Olivo airport, six miles northeast of Gela. Buffeted from their courses, the troop-carrying airplanes failed to reach the drop zone at the appointed times. Paratroops were strewn over a large area of southern Sicily, from Ponte Olivo to Niscemi, Vizzini, Ragusa, and as far east as Noto in the British Eighth Army sector.

At one minute past midnight on July 10, the I Armored Corps and Force 343 ceased to exist. The force commanded by General Patton was redesignated as the United States Seventh Army—"born at sea, baptized in blood," as it was so vividly characterized by its commander. Force 141 now became the Fifteenth Army Group (by the simple expedient of totaling the Seventh United States Army and the British Eighth).

Troops were scheduled to hit the beaches of Sicily less than three hours later, at 2:45 A.M. Earlier in the night the blazing Sicilian shores, target of naval fire and air strikes preceding the actual invasion, had come into view. Shortly after midnight the small boats of the sub-task forces started in. All landings had been successfully accomplished by 8:00 A.M.

Beginning at daybreak and continuing sporadically throughout the day, enemy aircraft strafed the beaches and transport areas. As early as 8:30 A.M., air observation reported enemy tanks moving in the direction of Gela, where the 1st Infantry Division was making the assault, and later reported making strikes on enemy tanks and trucks. By 9:45, two dozen enemy tanks—later identified as part of the Hermann Göring Divison— had driven to a point six miles to the northeast of Gela before they were stopped.

By the end of the day, however, all of the beachheads were secure, extending some two to four miles inland. More than 4,000 enemy prisoners had been taken.

Early on the morning of July 11, a major counterattack was launched against the Gela beachhead. Twenty German Mark IV tanks approached to within 2,000 yards of Gela before being stopped by artillery. At about 4:30 P.M. they renewed the engagement in another vicious counterattack. This time American forces had to call upon all means at hand—including naval gunfire, then a novelty against ground troops—to repel the advancing enemy force. But the enemy counterattack again fell short; by the end of the day another 4,300 enemy prisoners had been taken.

The enemy had tried unsuccessfully to defend at the water's edge as we had predicted. General Wedemeyer graciously stopped by the advance command post at his first brief respite. He visited only momentarily, just long enough to tell me, "You were right. The rest were wrong."

As American troops advanced inward from the beachheads, we got a rare but always hoped-for intelligence break. An enemy headquarters was captured in Gela. Hasty examination of the documents found there produced an Italian map that showed the locations of mine fields along the southern coast of the island and along coastal roads. We immediately had the map translated, and copies were sent to all divisions.

During the night of July 11-12, another lift of 82nd Airborne troops took off from Africa. Their transports suffered severe losses in flight, however, tragically shot down by Allied fire attracted by a German bomb run which had tied into the tail of one of the flights of C-47s. It was some time before the gunners learned that most of the air target had, in fact, been friendly and defenseless transports carrying American paratroops to their drop zones.

Meanwhile, the badly dispersed paratroops from the earlier drops had been trying valiantly to rejoin their units. We found ourselves with a new problem of immediate intelligence concern. Passwords and replies had been issued in Africa only for the initial period of landings, and additional ones were to be disseminated as soon as the command was rejoined. We realized that by the time the scattered paratroops could find their way back to units on the ground, the passwords and replies issued in Africa before embarkation would be invalid. All troops had to be notified of the situation and directed to be somewhat tolerant when challenging a suspected infiltrator—to accept with caution the older replies. No known casualties resulted.

With this lesson learned, however, we changed our policy. Passwords and replies were immediately issued for ten-day periods, ten days in advance of their intended use, with a directive that the dates of issue to various levels of command be staggered according to size of the command. Within corps they would be issued seven days in advance, within divisions five, regiments three, battalions two, and to companies the day before effective date. Individuals leaving their commands for more than twenty-four hours would be given the words which would regain them entrance to their area in advance.

Compromise through loss or misuse of the specified words was provided for by the availability of alternate words, which could be issued from a list prepared well in advance and placed under top secret control for immediate use on short notice. If the regular passwords were suspected to have been compromised, all users would be notified by prearranged code that certain alternates on the list would be used. We usually chose passwords which included sounds difficult for Germans to pronounce: the "th" in "thistle" for example, or the rolling "r" in "price."

On D-Day plus two, July 12, General Patton's command post was moved from the *U.S.S. Monrovia* to a school building in Gela. Patton himself, along with his command staff, moved into a grove east of town. The Seventh Army was now ashore to stay. Our intelligence preceding the invasion had been good and accurate. The enemy's initial defense of the beaches and attending counterattack to drive the Americans back into the sea had been accurately forecast. There had been no surprises.

*****

By D-Day plus six, July 16, operations had gone so well that the restless Patton was straining to drive beyond his assigned objectives. He sought and received permission to attack Agrigento and start his move to cut Sicily in half. But the permission carried some hampering provisos, including the condition that such an attack would not provoke a major battle. Thus Patton's forthright question to me: "If I attack Agrigento, will I bring on a major engagement?"

The query, succint as it was, implied a great many questions rolled into one: Is the enemy capable of taking a determined stand if I attack with my present troop strength and dispositions? Are his troop strength and dispositions such that I can expect to defeat him decisively, meanwhile keeping the engagement local in nature? Is he capable of offering so determined a defense that he might force me to bring in additional troops—ones now committed elsewhere or in reserve—to defeat him? Is he capable of bringing up reinforcements in such strength as to stage a general counteroffensive?

Also inferred by Patton were a great many other questions to which I was expected to know the answers: Will the characteristics of the terrain favor his defense or my attack, or will it be of equal favor to both of us? Will streams and rivers that are now fordable remain so? Or do weather forecasts indicate the probability of flash floods in the mountains, or of swollen, impassable streams?

In short, what General Patton really wanted me to tell him was my estimate of the enemy situation. What were the enemy capabilities?

Arguments over whether military intelligence forecasts should consider enemy *capabilities* or enemy *intentions* are probably as old as intelligence itself. The

American Army uses capabilities. No matter what the intentions of the enemy might be, he must have the capabilities to execute them; the converse is not true. He may have the capabilities and yet not execute them for reasons of his own. For intelligence purposes, only one thing counts: capabilities.

Our principles for determining enemy capabilities may be summed up with a brevity that denies their complexity: know your enemy, the terrain he controls, and the weather. In intelligence work, estimates of enemy strengths and dispositions are arrived at through a compilation of order of battle data; the terrain is determined through terrain studies and estimates, maps and models; the weather is forecast through climatic studies (and the current weather through latest forecasts). These factors go hand-in-hand, always together; they were the basic factors which I had to consider in answering General Patton's question. My negative response represented verbally the best estimate I could make of the situation at that time, based on all the known facts with any bearing on the situation, as gathered through the innumerable sources of intelligence.

To begin with, there was the simple matter of bookkeeping. We'd estimated enemy losses thus far in the campaign at 20,000 dead, wounded, and captured. Some sixty enemy tanks had been destroyed, along with more than 140 artillery pieces of seventy-five millimeter or larger. At least 112 enemy aircraft had been destroyed or captured.

There was evidence that the enemy—those who chose to stay and fight—was starting an eastward movement toward Messina under cover of stubborn rear action. Also of considerable interest to the G-2 Section was a report from Italian prisoners of war that their regard for the Germans was not too high. Italian troops, they complained, were always assigned the rear guard commands. When withdrawal was necessary, they often found that retreating Germans had laid mine fields behind, leaving the Italians in the unenviable position of having the German mine fields at their rear and advancing Americans at their front. Interrogation of German prisoners also revealed that the troop morale was low.

Intelligence information gathered since D-Day had painted an interesting day-by-day picture. The initial reaction to the invasion indicated that our forces had achieved a high degree of surprise. Except at isolated spots, the troops had met only light resistance along the beaches. Nor was any organized defensive system recognizable the following day. By D-Day plus two, the enemy still appeared to be fighting a delaying action, probably to allow time to fall back to higher ground inland. The Germans continued to attempt armored counterattacks, but these were repulsed. It now seemed apparent that the enemy, having failed in attempts to drive the invader back into the sea, would delay as long as possible to the north and east to permit full exploitation of the narrow Straits of Messina. Advancing American units were subject to intermittent light artillery fire during the day and met local counter-attacks spearheaded by tanks.

The enemy capability of most concern at the end of July 15 was the withdrawal of its main forces to the north and east, leaving delaying forces in contact and counterattacking with armor. The counterattacks would relieve relentless Seventh Army pressure then being exerted in the center of its area of advance and permit an enemy withdrawal either to the north or east. Some motor movement already had been observed in those directions.

The plottings on my improvised situation map showed the trends. After the initial major counterattack aimed at the landing beaches at Gela, withdrawal. Light resistance to the west. Patrol actions. The blowing of bridges. Concentration of troops for movement. The identification in combat of coastal division units whose primary training had been not for aggressive combat on the ground, but for defense of the coastline and resistance in the first stages of an invasion. Their mission was to prevent landings if possible, or at least to delay an invader until mobile units could arrive to counterattack. But no mobile groups had arrived to back them up.

If General Patton attacked Agrigento, would a major engagement result? In my view, it all boiled down to, "No, Sir." And we were right.

*****

During the night of July 17-18, with Agrigento now in American hands, the enemy withdrew from contact along the entire front. Mines and booby traps became the order of the day. Only 720 prisoners were taken on the eighteenth, as compared to thousands on previous days. At the same time, the Seventh Army, a force of more than 200,000 men, suffered only three killed, four missing, and 275 sick or wounded. Envelopment of Palermo was ordered, with the enemy to be driven north and east into the Messina area. There, we hoped, the troops massed by the enemy would be decimated while attempting to escape to the Italian mainland. The information gathered by my Seventh Army intelligence staff indicated the enemy would fight a defensive battle only, to ease its withdrawal.

On July 21, the advance command post of the Seventh Army headquarters was moved from Gela to Agrigento. General Keyes, in command of the provisional corps which had been activated in a divisional shift expressly for the campaign, advised Patton—disguising his message in recognizable American football terms—that if given the ball he could make a touchdown. Patton not only gave him the ball, but also told him to call the signals. Keyes's corps entered Palermo and accepted the surrender of enemy forces there on the twenty-second, ending the second rapid phase of the conquest of Sicily.

Prior to D-Day, the North African Reconnaissance Wing had produced a total of 195,000 aerial photographs and had assembled 1,400 mosaics for the invasion forces. Once Sicilian operations were underway a photo reconnaissance squadron of ten planes was placed in direct support of the Seventh Army. Up to D-Day plus ten the squadron was based in North Africa and crossed the Mediterranean twice daily on reconnaissance missions.

After the Gela airfield was captured, daily flights landed there for briefing and returned there upon completion of their missions. After the film was removed from their cameras for immediate developing and printing, however, the aircraft were returned to Tunisia to lessen the risk of damage or loss through the nightly enemy bomber attacks on the Sicilian airfields.

A total of 140 missions were flown with no losses during the thirty-eight days of Sicilian operations. Each sortie produced some 250 pictures which were printed in a standard nine-by-nine inch size for study by photo interpreters. A total of 86,000 prints were furnished during the campaign, on the basis of which forty-six photo-interpretation reports were issued.

Directly coupled with photo reconnaissance was the highly successful visual observation performed by observation squadrons flying pursuit, and by fighter-bomber aircraft. In Sicily, some of these planes were equipped with cameras capable of taking small, individual "spot" photographs, which proved extremely useful, confirming on film many of the visual observations made by the pilot during his limited time over critical areas. The enemy was seldom out of our sight.

*****

In the mop-up following the fall of Palermo, two high-ranking Italian officers were among those taken prisoner. The first was an army major general captured by troops of the 82nd Airborne Division near Trapani. After receiving documents taken from him, I asked that he be brought to the building where intelligence operations were going on.

By error, the Italian officer was brought directly to the room where I was busily comparing my own work map with unit designations and locations listed in a note-book that had been taken from him. Through an interpreter, I proceeded to question him. We soon learned that only a few days earlier he had been placed in command of the coastal division in the western part of the island. Recently transferred from the mainland, he had had no previous idea what his command would be. He had made up the notebook listing units of the command for his own benefit and was hardly oriented to the situation when the withdrawal commenced, so he could contribute nothing to the Allied intelligence picture. Noting the clearly visible intelligence work map on the wall, however, he told me he thought I knew more about his command than he did anyway.

He was correct.

The other highranking officer taken prisoner—also by the 82nd Airborne—was an admiral of the Italian Navy who was the predecessor of the general questioned earlier. He could add little to the intelligence picture, but spoke fluent English and had a great many questions of his own. Did I know so-and-so of the United States Navy? They were good friends. His last peacetime sea duty, he said, had been in Chinese waters and he had become friendly with a number of senior American Navy officers in that area. He was a great admirer of the United States and had no hard feelings against the Allies now.

Both of these officers professed a vehement anti-Fascism. Both seemed to feel that the war was a great mistake, although they said Mussolini had done a great deal of good for Italy in the beginning. It was when *Il Duce* allied himself with Hitler and began his plans for expansion beyond the Mediterranean that he lost the popular support of the Italian people. They told me sooner or later he also would lose the war.

*****

As the enemy continued to fight a delaying defensive war to protect the evacuation of its forces across the narrow Straits of Messina to the mainland, principal G-2 Section interest turned toward an evaluation of the defensive positions that would help the Italian and German troops in their flight. Enemy counterattacks had become more determined and there was more frequent demolition of bridges and critical roads. Our terrain studies showed that American forces would be pursuing the enemy across the most rugged of the Sicilian terrain.

Primarily, we were faced with the question of what positions the enemy would occupy once the evacuation movement started. They would, no doubt, defend and delay with strong points on successive ridges. With the terrain model built for planning in North Africa and carried along as operations progressed as a principal aid, my intelligence staff made a tactical terrain study.

As early as July 28 it had become clear to us that three particular ridges were likely defense lines. These ridges were designated as lines A, B, and C. Within days

```
From          :  172400B Jul 43
To            :  182400B Jul 43
Issuing Unit  :  Seventh Army
Place         :  In the Field
```

G-2 PERIODIC REPORT

No. 9

Map - G.S.G.S. 4164, 1:100,000, SICILY

1. ENEMY SITUATION AT END OF PERIOD.

a. Enemy front line: Situation in front of the Seventh Army on this date was of such fluid nature as to preclude the location of enemy front lines. Last contact was along general line SICLIA (G-4861) - North of S. CATERINA (H-0388) - North of ALGUARNERA (H-3578).

b. Defensive Organization: None, except large bivouac area north of S. CATERINA in vicinity of ENNA, and heavy artillery installations are reported Southeast of ENNA, vicinity H-2684.

c. Identifications (not previously reported): None.

2. ENEMY OPERATIONS DURING PERIOD.

a. General Summary: During the night of July 17/18, enemy withdrew from contact along the entire line, and only light resistance was offered to general advance of all units of the Seventh Army. A convoy estimated at one thousand troops with some tanks was reported moving east from H-1587 to H-1289.

3. MISCELLANEOUS.

a. Supplies and equipment: German PW states some difficulty being experienced with supplies due to rapid collapse of the Italian Army.

b. Concentrations: Enemy concentrations noted vicinity north of COMITINI (G-6866) and northwest of VILLAROSA (H-1588). It is believed that these concentrations are bivouac areas occupied preparatory to withdrawal to the north and west.

c. Minefields: Minefields and booby traps are being encountered with greater frequency along the entire front.

4. ENEMY CAPABILITIES.

(1) To defend along the general line ENNA (H28) - MUSSOMELI (G78) - BIVONA (G59) - CATTOLICA (G47).

(2) Same as (1) and counterattack against the west (left flank) with major Italian elements reinforced by German armor.

(3) To delay in successive positions along our general front to the north and west, with local counterattacks to relieve the pressure during withdrawal.

Capability (1) is favored. Italian reaction has been purely defensive. What aggressive action has been taken against this Army has been by German elements, which it is believed, with exception of portions (elements of the 15th Panzer Division) remaining in the ENNA - SAN CATERINA area, have been withdrawn along our front. A final defensive position will very likely be taken in the difficult terrain leading to the MESSINA peninsula, in an effort to either launch vigorous counterattack from that general direction at a later date or to permit withdrawal of German units to the Italian mainland. Sacrifice of the Italian troops in the west to fulfill that mission is indicated.

                                        KOCH
                                     AC of S, G-2

G-2 Periodic Report No. 9, U.S. Seventh Army operations in Sicily. (*U.S. Seventh Army Report of Operations*, "The Seventh Army in Sicily," October 1943) a German operations map was captured. Dated July 30, it marked the same three ridges as defensive phase lines A, B, and C!

Another German document dated August 2 fell into Seventh Army hands. It ordered the withdrawal of the Hermann Göring Division to line C on the night of August 2-3, leaving strong rear guards on line B to cover the move—a delay in successive positions. Not only had we analyzed the terrain identically, but our tactical thinking also had been the same as the Germans'.

The Seventh Army drive was now forcing the enemy steadily eastward. War-weary Italian forces still fighting on the northern flank were reinforced by the German 29th Motorized Division and they continued the defend and delay tactics. German aircraft carried out regular and precise bombing of the Palermo harbor.

Early August was marked by bloody combat; the Allied advance continued to be slow and tortuous. Meanwhile, the British were advancing up the east coast of the island, closing the vise which would leave escape to the toe of the Italian boot as the only way out for the fleeing enemy.

The enemy's dogged defend and delay tactics, strengthened by the natural fortifications of the rugged, mountainous terrain, led to a new kind of operation for the advancing Americans: seaward landings *behind* the enemy lines. Under a special operational directive issued August 3, a small amphibious task force was to land to the east of the enemy position and attack from the rear. A Navy task force and the XII Air Support Command would cooperate in both the landing and subsequent operations ashore. The beaches to be used had been covered in our preinvasion studies, which embraced the entire coast of Sicily.

We now made a complete re-analysis, based on up-to-date air photos. Drop zones for paratroops were established, possible mine fields were plotted, and pill boxes, machine guns, and anti-aircraft guns were pinpointed. Coastal defenses that were not yet overrun were indicated, as were wire entanglements, road blocks, and demolitions. Sea conditions—waves, surf, and swells—were studied. A new set of daylight and darkness tables was worked out. Anchorages and exits from the beaches were charted.

The results of the new studies were published August 5—two days after the directive—with accompanying photographs. The landing was made with complete surprise in the early morning darkness of August 8, our troops hitting the selected beaches without opposition. Some 1,500 prisoners were taken. A similar and completely successful attack was made August 11, again enveloping the enemy positions from the seaward side and supported by naval and air action.

Enemy evacuation across the Straits of Messina had gone on as rapidly as it could be accomplished. The intelligence information we had at hand indicated that

SAMPLE OF PSYCHOLOGICAL WARFARE BRANCH LEAFLETS

LA GUERRA CONTINUA

Gli alleati vi hanno ripetuto parecchie volte che per ottenere la pace l'Italia deve :

1) SBARAZZARSI DEL FASCISMO.

2) CESSARE DI AIUTARE LA GERMANIA.

Sebbene il regime fascista sia stato abbattuto, tuttavia il nuovo governo italiano continua ad aiutare i tedesch...

Il Presidente degli Stati Uniti ed il Primo Ministro del Regno Unito Britannico, si sono congratulati con il popolo italiano per l'essersi saputo sbarazzare dell'uomo che lo trascino nella guerra.

Il Generale Eisenhower promise che noi avremmo ridata la libertà alle centinaia di migliaia di prigionieri italiani catturati in Tunisia ed in Sicilia, qualora voi aveste impedito che i prigionieri alleati in Italia venissero trasferiti in Germania.

Gli Alleati speravano che il vostro nuovo governo avrebbe accettato queste condizioni onorevoli.

Per alcuni giorni dopo la caduta di Mussolini, gli Alleati sospesero i bombardamenti delle città italiane. Ora il vostro governo continua a combattere la guerra tedesca. Siamo perciò costretti a proseguire la guerra contro l'Italia con tutti i mezzi a nostra disposizione. Le città italiane saranno bombardate con maggiore intensità.

VOI SOLDATI ITALIANI CHE VI TROVATE IN QUESTO LEMBO DELLA SICILIA SARETE SCHIACCIATI COME LO FURONO LE POTENTI ARMATE DELL'ASSE IN TUNISIA.

Però il popolo italiano ripone tutte le speranze in voi Soldati d'Italia.

Se volete porre fine a questa inutile distruzione dovete agire in modo tale da costringere il vostro governo a rompere l'alleanza con la Germania Nazista.

Vi siete sbarazzati di Mussolini ! Noi crediamo fermamente che vi sbarazzerete pure dei tedeschi e salverete così l'Italia ed i suoi figli da una ulteriore distruzione e sacrificio inutile.

I Governi Alleati hanno offerto all'Italia il mezzo di ritirarsi dalla guerra. Il Popolo Italiano vuole, senza dubbio, accettare questa offerta.

Tuttavia la guerra continua......

A CHI LA COLPA ?

Translation of Italian Leaflet I. X.

(Front)

THE WAR CONTINUES

The Allies have repeatedly warned you that to obtain peace Italy must :

1. Get rid of Fascism.
2. Cease to aid Germany.

The Fascist regime has been overthrown but the new Italian Government continues to assist the Germans.

The President of the United States and the Prime Minister of Great Britain have congratulated the Italian people on having rid themselves of the man who dragged them into the war. General Eisenhower declared we would release the hundreds of thousands of Italian prisoners captured in Tunisia and Sicily provided your government prevented the Allied prisoners in Italy being transferred to Germany. The Allies hoped your government would accept these honourable conditions.

For some days after Mussolini's fall the Allies stopped bombing Italian towns. Now your government is continuing to fight Germany's war. Therefore we are compelled to continue the war against Italy, with all the means at our disposal. Italian cities will be bombed on an ever greater scale.

You, in this corner of Sicily, will be crushed as were the large Axis armies in Tunisia. The Italian people place all their hopes on you soldiers of Italy.

If you wish to put an end to this needless destruction you must act and speak so that your government is forced to break the alliance with Nazi Germany. You have got rid of Mussolini. We believe you can also get rid of the Germans, and so save Italy and her sons from further useless destruction and sacrifice !

The Allied governments have offered Italy a way out of the war. The Italian people want to accept this offer.

But the war continues......

WHO IS TO BLAME ?

SECRET

U.S. Seventh Army propaganda leaflet aimed at Italian soldiers and civilians in Sicily. (*U.S. Seventh Army Report of Operations*, "The Seventh Army in Sicily," October 1943)

(Front)

Translation of German Leaflet G. C.

C – 50

ITALY IS NOW AGAINST YOU

German Soldiers !
Here are the facts !
Facts which the whole world knows.
Are they known to you ?

ROME : Mussolini has been deposed. The Fascist Party has been officially dissolved. All Fascist emblems are being removed.

MILAN AND TURIN : Anti-Fascist organizations are taking over power in both cities. Revolutionary parties have seized control of all newspapers, public buildings, and communications. Striking workers have closed down the war plants. The Fascists are in hiding. Huge demonstrations demand a separate peace. Their cry is : " Throw the Germans out ! "

Swiss Border : The Gestapo is fleeing Italy. A German anti-aircraft battery was fired upon by an armed mob and disarmed. The Swiss authorities are refusing entry upon Swiss soil to fugitive Fascists.

PALERMO : American troops entering the capital were hailed by the inhabitants as liberators. They were greeted with flowers and wine.

BERLIN : When Hitler returned last week from his conference with Mussolini, he declared that Italy would remain true to the Axis. Once again, Der Fuehrer has been mistaken.

ITALIEN STEHT JETZT GEGEN EUCH

DEUTSCHE SOLDATEN !

Hier sind die Tatsachen !

Tatsachen, die die ganze Welt kennt.

Sind sie EUCH bekannt ?

ROM : Mussolini wurde gestuerzt. Die Faschistische Partei ist amtlich aufgeloest. Alle faschistischen Hoheitszeichen wurden entfernt.

MAILAND UND TURIN : Antifaschistische Organisationen uebernehmen in beiden Staedten die Macht. Revolutionaere Parteien haben saemtliche Zeitungen, oeffentliche Gebaeude und die Verkehrsmittel uebernommen. Streikende Arbeiter haben die Kriegslabriken stillgelegt. Die Faschisten verbergen sich. Massendemonstrationen ziehen durch die Strassen. Sie verlangen Separatfrieden. Ihr Ruf ist : Werft die Deutschen hinaus !

SCHWEIZER GRENZE : Die Gestapo verlaesst fluchtartig Italien. Eine deutsche Flak-Batterie wurde von der bewaffneten Menge beschossen und entwaffnet. Die Schweizer Behoerden verweigern den gefluechteten Faschisten den Uebertritt auf schweizerischen Boden.

PALERMO : Die in die Hauptstadt einrueckenden amerikanischen Truppen wurden von der ganzen Bevoelkerung als Befreier umjubelt. Mit Blumen und Wein wurden sie begruesst.

BERLIN : Als Hitler in der letzten Woche von seiner Unterredung mit Mussolini zurueckkehrte erklaerte er, dass Italien der Achse treu bleiben wird. Der Fuehrer hat sich wieder einmal geirrt.

U.S. Seventh Army propaganda leaflet aimed at German soldiers in Sicily. (*U.S. Seventh Army Report of Operations***, "The Seventh Army in Sicily," October 1943)**

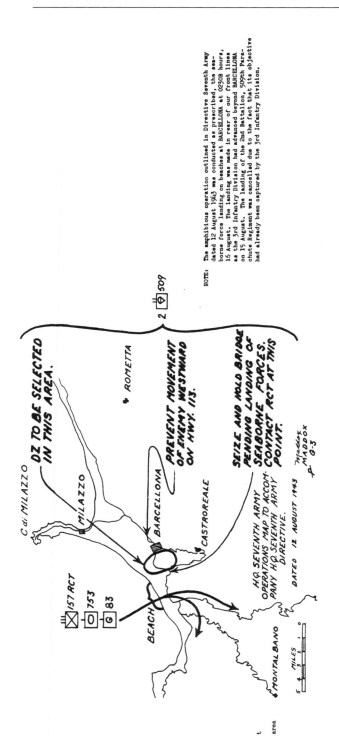

NOTE: The amphibious operation outlined in Directive Seventh Army
        dated 12 August 1943 was conducted as prescribed, the sea-
        borne force landing on beaches at BARCELLONA at 0230B hours,
        16 August. The landing was made in rear of our front lines
        as the 3rd Infantry Division had advanced beyond BARCELLONA
        on 15 August. The landing of the 2nd Battalion, 509th Para-
        chute Regiment was cancelled due to the fact that its objective
        had already been captured by the 3rd Infantry Division.

SECRET

U.S. Seventh Army operations map for behind-the-lines amphibious landing in Sicilian campaign. (*U.S. Seventh Army Report of Operations,* "The Seventh Army in Sicily," October 1943) the transfer of 400 guns or vehicles and more than 10,000 troops could be accomplished each night. We estimated that the bulk of the German forces had reached the Italian mainland by August 12. The absence of enemy contact clearly indicated that the Axis forces contemplated no further defense of Sicily, although Messina itself might continue to be held as a fortress by Italian troops the Germans had left behind.

Final withdrawal took place on the night of August 16-17, however, and at mid-morning Patton entered Messina. Organized resistance on the island had ended. The only enemy capabilities on Sicily now were those of sabotage and spot raids, either naval or commando.

Thirty-eight days after the initial assault, the Allied campaign for Sicily ended. General Patton's command post, which had been moved frequently as the Seventh Army drove across the island, was returned without delay to Palermo. We'd learned important lessons in intelligence activities. Most important, no errors of significance—significance in terms of lives lost—had been made.

5

OPERATION OVERLORD

By October, combat troops of the Seventh Army were already assigned to and fighting as part of the United States Fifth Army in Italy or were earmarked for and en route to the United Kingdom for the cross-channel invasion of France. With Seventh Army Headquarters relatively inactive, General Patton made a number of well-planned personal appearances in various Mediterranean areas. Such trips were designed, in great measure, to keep the enemy guessing: Did his visit to Corsica indicate a study of potential airfields and ports for use in the invasion of southern France? Was his visit to the Polish Brigade in Egypt a forerunner to an Allied invasion of the Balkans?

While press dispatches always described the Patton visits after they had occurred (just in case the watching eyes and listening ears of the enemy should miss one), the advanced planning was super-secret. For the Corsica junket Patton and a very limited staff group would depart Palermo in an unarmed C-47 and be joined by General Alphonse Juin of the recently reconstituted French Army and his comparably small staff at a small and inconspicuous airfield in North Africa. The party would total about ten persons. None of the staff members had been told of the detailed arrangements. Their airplane was to be picked up by two fighter escorts off Sardinia and accompanied in at Ajaccio, the Corsican capital, at 11:00 A.M. Plans were changed in flight, however, and the group landed ten minutes early; by eleven o'clock they were well away from the field. At precisely 11:00 A.M. the Germans bombed the field for the first time in days. Was it sheer coincidence, or had there been a security breach? We never knew the answer.

The period was one of relative calm for our staff. With future Seventh Army plans unannounced, we could not plan for specific objectives. Employing the time available, the G-2 team undertook studies which would be of value should any target in the Mediterranean become the Seventh Army's next objective. Made just as carefully as "for the record" assignments, our studies assumed a sea-borne invasion would be launched and considered all potential areas. Navy and air planners participated, with completed plans war-gamed and enemy orders of battle kept up to date. Realistic limitations were imposed on us, however, including availability of naval craft and the extent to which air cover could be provided.

To profit from the experiences of Sicily (and also North Africa, for most Seventh Army staff members were now veterans of two invasions), the chief of staff directed all staff sections to prepare outlines of their respective planning activities, duties, and responsibilities. In the G-2 Section, we decided that this would be presented as a job analysis, not only for information but also for use in the future guidance of the section and in the orientation of new personnel. It would have to be all-embracing, yet flexible, a "G-2 planning plan" which would show in detail how to plan for all intelligence responsibilities in joint operations.

The emerging blueprint for combat intelligence planning, adaptable to units of almost any size, set day-to-day goals during a prescribed period before a major new offensive. At the same time, it provided a ready check list by which an intelligence staff could measure its progress. It was to prove fundamentally sound in later use for the commitment of the Third Army in Normandy and the Seventh Army in southern France, as well as for the planning of occupational duties in a defeated Germany early in 1945.

Actually, the plan was to be called into play shortly after completion—although not as a Seventh Army activity. General Patton was relieved of his command on January 1, 1944. Meanwhile, the Allied Force headquarters had called for a planning staff from Seventh Army headquarters to begin work on invasion planning for southern France—Operation "Anvil." The planning staff left Palermo and, traveling by an improvised rail route to Siracusa and then across to Algiers, arrived in the suburb of Bouzareah on January 12. The unit was designated Force 163, a tag once again derived from a room number.

Intelligence problems, we believed, would be relatively simple, but Anvil was caught between operations in progress in Italy and the planned cross-channel invasion of France. The actual forces available to the operation were unknown. Fortunately, through the previous studies of assumed sites for activity by the Seventh Army, much of the groundwork had already been laid. Planning was still based on assumptions; the invasion site was still not affirmed. But by the end of January the drafts of broad directives for intelligence training of component units had been developed and the essential intelligence information we needed was at hand. Studies and research material were beginning to appear; a preliminary G-2 estimate of the enemy situation was completed. Our intelligence operation, despite handicaps, was progressing on schedule.

Several of the veteran staff planners of Force 163 had departed by mid-February, leaving at the rate of one or two a week. Their destinations were not revealed. No one asked. Rumor had it that Major General Alexander M. Patch had, since Patton's departure, become the Seventh Army commander-designate and was en route from the Pacific. He would be accompanied by some members of his own staff. Rumor also had it that Patton was in England awaiting a new mission.

*****

On February 22, I received secret orders, effective three days later, relieving me from further assignment and duty with the Seventh Army and assigning me to a new command in the European theater of operations. The imposing set of orders authorized travel "by military, naval, commercial aircraft, belligerent, naval vessel, commercial steamship, Army transport, and/or rail." I elected air transport.*

Flying by way of Casablanca on a cold and moonless night, our plane landed early in the morning at Prestwick, Scotland. Orders awaiting me there directed that I proceed to Knutsford, England. Just outside town, in ancient Peover Hall, I found Patton's headquarters.

Although a closely-kept secret at this time, picturesque Peover Hall was soon to become headquarters of the Third United States Army, the new Patton command. Integrated into the Third Army staff would be a number of the old Sicilian Seventh Army staff officers. As Patton himself would say in an address of welcome to members of the main body of the staff arriving from Fort Sam Houston, Texas, on March 23, *two* old headquarters—each with its own procedures and one with the advantage of combat experience—were being merged to form a *third* army headquarters. Taking advantage of the best of each, he hoped the new combination would function even better than its predecessors had individually.

Shortly after my arrival in England, I was called for by the Army commander. General Patton was standing, bent over, alongside a table against the inner wall. His elbows and forearms were resting on a spread Michelin roadmap of France, the

* I was authorized to have my faithful companion and driver, Technician Third Class Carmen DeJohn (again promoted as several times before on a change of station order) to proceed by sea to rejoin me in the new assignment.

type automobile clubs the world over provide for their members. Glancing sideways, the general straightened up and asked me to join him at the table. His finger continued to rest on the map.

"Koch," he said, "I want all of your G-2 planning directed to here."

I bi-focaled my glasses and looked. General Patton's finger rested deep in France. On Metz! Then, starting at Nantes on the Atlantic coast and sweeping his finger along the Loire River toward the east, the commander continued, "I do not intend to go south of the Loire unless it is necessary to avoid a right-angled turn."

In broadest terms, Patton had just stated his EEIs—Essential Elements of Information—for the planned Third Army offensive on the European continent. Although I didn't know it then, he had just concluded what was to be his only personally-expressed intelligence directive, not only for the cross-channel invasion in Operation "Overlord," but for the rest of the Third Army's operations in Europe until the war's end.

The task facing my intelligence staff was now clear. Anything which might affect the Third Army mission, from the coast of France all the way to Metz by way of a circuitous route through Brittany, was now of critical concern. Initially, the commander would want to know what to expect upon arrival on the Continent in terms of enemy opposition, the terrain, and the weather. From then on he would want to be kept abreast of the details of these and other factors, well in advance, as operations proceeded.

Shortly after I'd received Patton's initial directive, the Third Army was directed to prepare five alternate plans to insure gaining a foothold in France if the lodgement area, at the base of the Cherbourg Peninsula, planned for the main offensive, had for any reason not been secured by the First Army. The selected areas included a great portion of the Atlantic coastal perimeter to the west of the Cherbourg Peninsula in the general areas of St. Malo, St. Brieuc, Morlaix, Brest, and Vannes. The operations would be joint in nature: assaults over the beaches in a coordinated attack with ground, air, and naval forces participating. Which, if any, of the plans would be used would have to be decided after the initial invasion had been launched in Normandy.

The resultant EEIs which we published in May had to be all-inclusive, embracing the collection of all intelligence information necessary to meet the requirements of any of the missions under consideration. We had to make all our collection efforts concurrently and all troops, seasoned or new, had to be alerted to the type of information that was desired as soon as it was available.

What the commander needed to know about each area was: What is the extent and nature of enemy naval defenses and activity in this area? What is the nature, extent, disposition and status of the enemy ground forces and defenses? What is the nature, extent, disposition and status of the enemy air and anti-aircraft defenses? What are the specific topographic, meterological and hydrographic factors which affect our mission? What is the status of the public utilities? And what is the civilian attitude?

These basic questions constituted the Third Army's initial EEIs as issued while we were in the United Kingdom. Broken down into specifics, they covered thirty main subdivisions with a total of more than two hundred items on which reports had to be ready as soon as possible to support the plans for the six different operational missions possible.

For example, asking about the extent and nature of enemy naval defenses and activities in the area led to specific additional questions concerning such items as the number, type, and condition of captured or salvaged craft, the number, type, location, and effectiveness of German naval units, and the status of training and the morale of the crews. What types, to what extent, and what means of offshore gunfire protection were employed? How were underwater defenses controlled? What were the types of obstructions used under water, in ports, on the beaches—wire, mines? And what was the number, type, direction, and time of enemy movements by sea and close-in inland waterways?

Each of the other basic EEIs carried implications for a similar array of items about which we had to obtain specific, detailed information. When full answers were found, or when the choice of areas was narrowed, the separate questions would be dropped from the list, reducing the Essential Elements of Information to those still current.

Of the initial EEIs, those referring to the enemy ground forces and defenses accounted for the greatest number of questions. But those regarding naval defensive capabilities and air potential and anti-aircraft defenses, and those affecting available topographic, meteorological, and hydrographic data contributed their fair share. Some of the items included were of more direct concern to higher headquarters and had been passed to the Third Army G-2 Section for collection.

I knew that General Patton, commanding an invading force, would be interested initially in the enemy naval defenses, the coast and beach defenses (including the type and quality of troops to be expected), and, once the landing sites were disclosed, the enemy's ability to reinforce in those areas by land or air and to keep our follow-up reinforcements from reaching France from the United Kingdom by sea.

It was a large order. But intelligence officers of all Third Army units, many facing the enemy for the first time, were apprised of what detailed information was necessary to satisfy the EEIs—what to look for. All were told what they, within their commands, might be able to contribute in the search for military information by piecemeal, methodical collection and timely reporting. Acquiring such vital information and keeping it current, we reemphasized, was their G-2 responsibility.

Intelligence problems presented by the Third Army needs were similar, though not identical, to those faced by "oldtimers" on the staff before. The G-2 planning plan devised by the Seventh Army staff in Sicily had stood the test in the Mediterranean. It would serve its purpose again, although it now had to be modified somewhat to meet differences in administrative methods between the North African and European theaters of operation.

Although the newly-arrived members of the G-2 Section had been fully trained in combat intelligence practices in the States, our reorganization in England emphasized activities that Stateside training normally would not provide. We stressed the importance and technical requirements of the duties of "G-2 Air" (by this time a formally recognized staff section responsible for air reconnaissance and observation), the direct relationship with the Counter Intelligence Corps in combat operations, and the great number of auxiliary agency functions.

*****

The new intelligence planning staff assembled for the first time on March 25. The Third Army, it was announced, would be used in the coming invasion as a follow-up force with second priority. It would follow over the beaches or ports secured by the First Army with a time lag of thirty days. All our planning would be phased accordingly, lagging thirty days behind a projected but unknown invasion date. Although there was no indication of what that date might be, it appeared we would have several months for planning. It was decided that the Third Army's G-2 planning would be worked out on the assumption we had at least ninety days in which to complete our work.

G-2 Section conferences were held every fifth calendar day. Following each of these, we wrote a memorandum concerning progress made and critical problems still unsolved and sent it to the chief of staff for his information. The first of eighteen such reports was submitted on April 4, twelve days after the main headquarters landed in the United Kingdom.

In those dozen days we had prepared a preliminary intelligence estimate, mostly for the benefit and orientation of the G-2 branch chiefs. We felt they would then be better able to align themselves with the tactical thinking and direct their own branch efforts with greater understanding. A terrain analysis of Brittany was prepared by our staff. Maps for planning were requisitioned. Censorship guidances were revised as applicable in the United Kingdom.

Some of the specialists arrived during this period—an order of battle team, a photo-interpreter team, and a CIC detachment. Arrangements were made to have OSS and Signal Intelligence Service representatives available. We also initiated steps for basic air coverage of the entire area of Brittany.

No terrain model makers were available, so a strategic terrain model scaled 1:250,000 was undertaken locally with borrowed engineer personnel under direct supervision of the G-2 Section. Photo mosaics requested were received and sent to various units for training purposes. All planning supplies were requisitioned. A directive for the supervision of intelligence training in all elements of the command was approved.

The headquarters war room had been opened on March 27. A month later, on April 29, the complete G-2 plan for the Third Army's overall Overlord mission was ready. The corps commanders had been briefed. A complete terrain model of Brittany was in full use. We had arranged to obtain First Army's passwords and replies to keep them identical until Third Army became operational on the Continent. We had established a map policy and planning maps, bundled and made secure, had been delivered.

Initial sets of 150 prints of basic photo reconnaissance coverage arrived, and with them came information that a minimum of two weeks' notice would be necessary to fulfill additional requests for photo coverage flown from the United Kingdom. And quite properly so, since first priority for these facilities was given to the D-Day invaders of the First Army.

Advanced planning had been undertaken for the creation of the Third Army Information Service. This service, for which the 6th Cavalry Group under command of Colonel Edward M. "Joe" Fickett was selected, would monitor radio traffic from the friendly battalions through regiments, divisions, and reconnaissance units. It would establish officer patrol front-line contacts with the headquarters of all battalions and regiments to exchange information. It would report directly to the Third Army advance command post, bypassing normal communications, to be optionally monitored by intermediate headquarters. Timely reporting would be its greatest concern. It would help Patton's headquarters keep him apprised of the location of units and contacts with the enemy, and pass along all unevaluated intelligence information it could get.

On May 8, six weeks after arrival in the United Kingdom, Third Army's D-Day minus fifty-five, the complete intelligence plan for Operation Overlord was published. By D-minus thirty, maps of the perimeter of Brittany—from the Cherbourg Peninsula around the coast of France to the mouth of the Loire River—were on hand. Map coverage of the interior of Brittany was about eighty percent complete. G-2 estimates were kept current, as were photo-interpreter reports of fortifications at focal points around the perimeter. We obtained photography for artillery training, and we completed special studies of all beaches which might be used.

Our basic photo coverage expanded gradually to ninety percent of the perimeter and ninety-three percent of the areas of immediate concern in the interior of Brittany. A scale model of Belle Isle in Quiberon Bay, near the mouth of the Loire, was completed for the study of the Atlantic approaches in case the overall invasion events would require its neutralization and use by Third Army. Surveys of linguists were undertaken. A sampling of two corps and five divisions produced sixty-five officers and 431 enlisted men who claimed fluency in German and sixty-two officers and 372 enlisted men who could act as interpreter-translators for their units in French.

Preliminary arrangements made for the organization of an army photo center were bearing fruit. Photo-interpreter teams would initially report to the G-2 Section at Third Army headquarters for orientation and then be dispatched to the airfield for work. On a reduced scale, the photo center started its operations in England at Chalgrove. Three officers were detailed there from the air section to assist in its growing interests. An additional experienced Seventh Army officer, an expert in the still scarce photo-interpretation techniques, reported from the Mediterranean. We held conferences with the XIX Tactical Air Command's director of reconnaissance to establish procedures and lay future plans.

We then had to undertake more detailed terrain studies, covering such subjects as inundated areas or those subject to inundation, pinpointing the locations of marshes and swamps. Planners were constantly vigilant for areas unsuitable for the use of tanks, or areas which might limit or impede cross-country mobility. "Trafficability" maps were prepared, showing the weight-carrying capacities of terrain for cross-country purposes. A G-2 officer attended daily noon briefings given by General Bradley's First (later Twelfth) United States Army Group headquarters in London. Town plans and Michelin Guides were distributed to the command. We published *Third Army G-2 Estimate No. 4* on June 5, D-Day minus twenty-four in terms of the G-2 planning plan.

News of the Normandy invasion broke by radio broadcast early the next day. General Patton hastily summoned to his quarters those of his staff then in the building, and while listening to the news over his radio proposed a toast to an early and speedy victory. Chapel bells in nearby Knutsford rang out the joy of the British.

Which of the plans developed would be used to commit the Third Army on the Continent? This was the question foremost in the minds of all the planners.

On June 17, *Third Army G-2 Estimate No. 5* was issued. It would be the last before Patton's command became operational across the channel. Incoming reports told of the invasion's progress and listed new enemy identifications. At Third Army headquarters, enemy reaction to the assault was of particular interest because the final selection of the plan for Third Army employment on the Continent hinged on this crucial factor.

Limited distribution had been made of an analysis which would become the first formal *G-2 Weekly Report* and later a weekly supplement to the daily *G-2 Periodic Report*. Titled "Significant Order of Battle Facts," it carried only two headings: "Significant Facts" and "Conclusions." It had been prepared for a special briefing of General Patton.

Based on intelligence reports covering the first ten days of the invasion, the first section of the report pointed out that two enemy infantry divisions had been moved from Brittany to the Carentan area and another had been withdrawn from the Isle of Jersey. The 1st SS Panzer Division had moved from Antwerp on June 8 and had been committed on the beachhead front; another Panzer unit had been identified north of Paris as one which had probably left the Russian front in May. The 2nd SS Panzer Division had moved from Toulouse near the Spanish border to Mayenne on June 13. As of June 17, a total of sixteen and a half German divisions were in contact with Allied invasion troops, four Panzer and four infantry divisions were moving, and one division had not yet been identified. Of greater immediate concern to Patton was the fact that the major entrance to the port of Cherbourg, which might have been used in the Third Army mission, was already blocked by sunken ships. Its seaplane base and some harbor installations had been destroyed.

Enemy strength had not been nearly so great as we had originally estimated, however. Movement of troops out of Brittany might leave only a thin crust of German defenders to face the Third Army, and strategic reserves seemed to be on the move. The overall success of the invasion to date indicated that the Third Army would not have to follow through on any of its alternate plans. Although Cherbourg would not be available for debarkation, Omaha and Utah beaches would be. This lodgement area into which Third Army troops would be infiltrated and from which they would begin the planned sweeping operations had been secured by the First Army.

*****

General Patton always kept a special map of the immediate area of operations at hand. Uniquely folded, covered, and waterproofed, and about ten by twenty inches in size, it accompanied him on all of his travels. Scaled to about eight miles to the inch, it contained more important towns and crossroads with secret code identification numbers. By referring to these he could keep his headquarters staff informed as to where he was or what he wanted done. Four identical copies were always made—one for General Patton, one for his chief of staff, one for his signal officer, and one for me.

In the early planning days for Overlord, a G-2 Section newcomer had prepared the special map and delivered it personally to General Patton in the commander's office. Patton looked it over carefully.

"This is fine," he said with a twinkle in his eye. "But it only goes as far east as Paris. I'm going to Berlin."

6

OPPORTUNITY KNOCKS

Late in July, 1944, in a tent in the *bocage* country of Normandy fifteen miles south of Cherbourg and eight miles behind the front lines of VIII Corps, a press briefing was in progress. The arrival of the Third Army on the Continent—indeed, the fact that such an army even existed—was still top secret. The newsmen, of course, knew.

"General," one of the correspondents asked, "could you tell us when the Third Army will become operational?"

"I could," General Patton replied, "but I *can't.*" It was a matter of security.

Not only was planned activation of the Third Army on the Continent one of the war's most closely guarded secrets, but it also was part of a classic Allied deception. Before, during, and after the June invasion, the Allies had maintained a fictitious radio traffic which would indicate the presence of a United States Army group in southeast England opposite the Pas-de-Calais. The enemy apparently intercepted these communications as planned and obligingly accepted the fact that such a force actually existed.

Knowing that the Pas-de-Calais area represented the shortest cross-channel route for a main effort toward the Ruhr and the heart of Germany, Hitler believed that the Normandy invasion was a feint to draw his major forces to the west, and that a major Allied assault would be made at the Pas-de-Calais. Further, he was convinced that it was Patton (whom the Germans had long before learned to respect and fear) who would command this new Allied assault and open a second beachhead. To further the deception and add as much confusion as possible to the enemy's intelligence picture, the Allies reconstituted Bradley's First Army Group as the Twelfth. The First, on paper, remained in England.

Though the weary German Seventh Army opposing American forces in the area of St. Lô repeatedly called for critically needed replacements, Hitler held his Fifteenth Army with its eighteen divisions inactive behind the Pas-de-Calais, waiting for the Patton invasion which never came. The reserve finally was loosed on July 25, but it provided too little, too late for the heavily engaged German forces. On that same day the United States First Army broke through at St. Lô.

A few days later, the censorship wraps were removed. The Third Army became operational at noon on August 1, Patton's troops pouring into the Allied battle for France.

It was an intricate maneuver from the outset. Down the west coast of the Cotentin (Cherbourg) Peninsula, troops of two Third Army corps streamed simultaneously through a narrow corridor to get "around the corner"—west into Brittany, south toward the Loire, and east toward Le Mans. Two main north-south coastal highways were the only routes available, and these converged at the Avranches bridge to form a single roadway for a distance of about five miles. It would become known, appropriately, as the "Avranches Gap."

To the east, a part of the First Army was holding the landward shoulder against a determined German enemy.

On August 3, the *Third Army G-2 Periodic Report* noted that, on the immediate front, the enemy was capable of defending to the south while attempting to organize a major counterattack toward the west. Uncertainty of the location of four Panzer divisions, known to be in the vicinity, created a potential threat against the Third Army landward flank.

"Such a concentration," opined the report, "would give the enemy a force capable of being used in a major counterattack aimed at driving a wedge to the Channel between our North and South forces. Such severence would rupture the jugular supply vein of our Southern columns, rendering them logistically inoperative."

The southernmost columns were, by this time, well on their way into Brittany. To have them cut off now would create a critical situation. Where were the Panzer divisions in question? When and where did the enemy plan to use them?

Awakened at 2:00 A.M. on August 7 by the intelligence section duty officer, I got the answers. Word had just been received from higher headquarters, I was informed, that a "usually reliable source" had reported that a German counterattack of major proportions against the First Army was imminent. The First Army had been informed.

I fumblingly got into my clothes in blackout and groped my way to Colonel Maddox's tent.* We discussed the situation. The First Army could no doubt withstand the attack, but if by sheer weight of effort the Germans could breach the wall, Third Army troops that were already through the gap would be pinched off. Although this assuredly would be only a temporary situation, they would be in jeopardy of being in a logistically untenable position. We agreed that although nothing *might* happen we should immediately arouse and inform the chief of staff, General Gay.

In the latter's van, I presented the enemy situation as it then stood. All the "if's" and "and's" were presented. Maddox noted that the XX Corps was now moving south through the gap and that one of its divisions, the 35th, was opposite the critical point. If the 35th were halted and turned toward the east, he suggested, it would be in a position to backstop the First Army at the most threatened and most critical points.

"We'll go see the commander," Gay decided.

Patton's van was not far away. He, too, was awakened and informed of the situation. After a few minutes' discussion, he directed immediate verbal orders to the XX Corps to make plans to attack in anticipation of a strong German counterattack on Avranches.

The German counterattack came as expected. The 35th Division, later attached to the VII Corps of the First Army for that action, became heavily engaged. Third Army troops continued to pour through the gap. The all-out German counterattack was not only repulsed, but the stage was set for the encirclement of the entire German Seventh Army in the Falaise area, one hundred miles west of Paris.

With Montgomery's forces closing in from the north and Patton's Third Army moving up rapidly from the south, the enemy was in a desperate situation. When Third Army troops reached Argentan, their immediate objective, the fifteen-mile Argentan-Falaise gap remained as the only escape route for the Germans. Patton wanted to push on quickly and close the gap, but higher headquarters, fearing the possible head-on collision of American and British units and feeling Patton's troops might be spread too thin, denied his request. Thousands of enemy soldiers escaped the trap.

*****

To a retreating enemy, Patton's forces now became the pursuer. The Third Army struck swiftly at the flank of the fleeing German forces, capturing Le Mans and
_____
* Halley Maddox, who had served as the Seventh Army operations officer, also was among those joining Patton's Third Army staff in their old positions.

driving north to create and close the gap between Alençon and Falaise. This drive created a long, open flank along the Loire to the south, held by only enough troops to patrol the river and deny crossing to Germans then trapped south of it. The flank was kept under constant visual air reconnaissance and surveillance by the XIX Tactical Air Command. This, augmented by ground reports from French forces operating in the area, resulted in continuous pinpointing of German movement. If a threat should develop, we would meet it without delay.

Reports persisted that the 11th Panzer Division, previously reported in southern France, was moving to the north to reinforce battered German elements there. If so, it could pose a threat to the Third Army's rapid pursuit of the enemy. Visual air reconnaissance of considerable scope and high priority was undertaken. Methodical search of the area south of the Loire failed to show any trace of the suspected division, but day-to-day surveillance was continued until 11th Panzer troops were identified in contact with the United States Seventh Army moving up the Rhone valley after its invasion on the Mediterranean coast.

The watchful eye of the TAC also detected large-scale foot, rail, and motor traffic moving to the north and east in the area south of the Loire as the enemy sought to escape a closing Allied trap. These movements were taken under air attack, the TAC assuming responsibility not only for detecting these mass enemy movements, but also for interrupting them.

To the north, meanwhile, Third Army troops had established bridgeheads on the Seine and advanced so rapidly on Paris that a planned air drop proved unnecessary. Paris fell to the Allies on August 25.

With the Allied plan now calling for a general advance toward the Rhine, the Third Army advanced along a ninety-mile front toward the northeast. This, coupled with the extended southern flank along the Loire, gave Patton's forces a combined flank and front of some 450 miles. Two corps drove toward Metz and Nancy in what was to be a major thrust toward the Moselle.

It had become obvious by this time that, unless the enemy was successful in desperate efforts to the contrary, the Third Army soon would join forces with the Seventh Army advancing up from the south. Hitler, again revealing a respect and fear for Patton over and above that normally shown for the Allies in general, determined to launch a counteroffensive to slow or stop the Third Army advance—even if doing so meant lessened support of the frantic German efforts to build stable defensive positions on the Siegfried Line. A limited counterattack was begun by the 112th Panzer Brigade, which was quickly defeated by French ground forces supported by the XIX TAC. Although some units were heavily engaged, the Third

Army drive was not stopped. The Third and Seventh armies met in mid-September, crushing the German 16th Division between them.

German forces south of the Loire, with no hope of extricating themselves and under constant watch by TAC air surveillance, marched northward under flags of truce. On September 18, surrender was arranged for more than 19,000 enemy soldiers.

General Patton asked to be relieved of the acceptance of their surrender (the Germans reportedly had asked that they be allowed to surrender to him). Lieutenant General William H. Simpson, commander of the newly-activated Ninth Army, asked Major General O. P. Weyland, XIX TAC commander, to be present. The invitation was an acknowledgement of the Tactical Air Command's contribution in forcing the surrender, a high tribute to the success of joint ground-air operations.

Our intelligence section, meanwhile, had kept in mind the directive issued by Patton early in March in the United Kingdom—that intelligence planning be directed toward Metz. Exactly three months after that directive, Third Army reconnaissance troops entered the bastioned city but were forced to withdraw.

Despite Patton's continued protests, his entire army was forced by a decision of the high command to settle down along what roughly approximated static lines on the Moselle to await a general straightening out of the front. Problems of supply had grown acute and the cessation of major offensive operations would give logistics an opportunity to catch up. Reluctantly, Patton turned his attention to areas where limited offensive movement might eliminate some of the stronger pockets of enemy resistance, or deny the enemy opportunity to constitute new ones. We hoped such action would help clear a path of advance once the "green light" for the offensive was received.

The G-2 Section undertook a comprehensive study of the Metz fortifications, a historical analysis to be accomplished in the field under blackout conditions. The liberation of Paris in August had made available French files and archives with maps and studies of the area, all of which we considered in this unusual effort.

Metz, a bastion of defense, had figured prominently in the history of previous wars in Europe. Surrendered by France in the Franco-Prussian War in 1870, it had been re-taken by French and American troops in 1918 and captured again by German forces in 1940. Its capture had been by siege, however, the city's heavy fortifications making it virtually immune to direct assault.

Our new intelligence studies led to a series of briefings, General Patton and other members of his staff listening attentively to our descriptions of the defense capabilities of the Maginot Line, built by the French to face the east but now—in the hands of those it was designed to defend against—facing west instead. The commander accepted our intelligence recommendations for a general attack plan against the modernized nineteenth century installations, applying 1944 weaponry, mobility, and air power.

The restraining order which had stopped the Third Army drive was lifted in November. Metz and the twenty-odd forts in its area became the primary objective of Patton's XX Corps. The offensive jumped off on November 8; Metz was taken on the eighteenth. Patton's troops had succeeded in taking the city by direct assault, the first time it had fallen to such a tactic since 451 A.D.

All organized resistance in the area ceased by November 21. The various forts were then reduced individually, some bypassed to "die on the limb," others stubbornly resisting until taken by final assault. The last, "Jeanne d'Arc," surrendered on December 14.

*****

After Metz was occupied by American forces, a lone enemy agent was apprehended there. He was a young man—almost boyish in appearance—whose native French loyalties had changed to German through the years of occupation of his homeland. He had been surreptitiously dropped, radio-equipped, from a German airplane under cover of darkness on a moonless night.

The young agent had never ridden in an airplane until that fateful night, when he parachuted from a blacked-out craft into a strange area. On alighting, he failed to recognize the landmarks of his appointed place as they had been described to him. The plane undoubtedly was off course, but he had not been told. He was completely lost.

Roaming aimlessly around the city, suitcase in hand, he was soon taken into custody. He readily admitted his disgust for the whole operation; he was ready to quit.

We asked him if he wanted to help the Allied cause—that of his homeland.

He would, and gladly. But how?

By simply following the instructions he had received and transmitting his messages to Germany as he was expected to do, we told him.

Again, he readily agreed.

The first message the young agent received directed him to report the vehicular bumper markings of the American units which were then passing through Metz. He did this, his report provided by Americans who painstakingly copied the markings as the vehicles passed the selected point. No harm done; that miscellany of markings would be practically indecipherable even to American intelligence.

Next, the young Frenchman was directed to make a personal reconnaissance for the reception of another German agent, routing the newcomer from an area nearby, to the heart of the city. This request, too, was complied with—not by him but *for* him, by American personnel. More such reconnaissances were ordered and made, all faithfully reported by radio to his superiors. Finally, he was directed to be prepared to assist a number of other agents who would be dropped at certain hours, at certain places, all detailed in his secret radio traffic.

The newcomers arrived on schedule, and were dutifully received by American reception committees. It took us two days to locate one stray.

Meanwhile, the original agent had been advised by radio that, "For his devotion to duty . . . for his excellent work . . . for the Fatherland," he had been awarded the Iron Cross!

*****

The German 17th SS Panzer Grenadier Division had, by October, become one of Third Army's "favorites." Whenever it appeared, things were bound to happen. When it broke contact, things were bound to happen elsewhere. A feeling of closeness with the division had developed in the G-2 Section. There was always a profound interest in where it was, what it was doing, and how well it was getting along (and, if out of contact, where it would turn up next). All of our intelligence collection agencies were constantly on the alert to keep abreast of its activities. It was a fighting outfit.

The 17th SS one day would provide the perfect example of what *not* to do, however, from the standpoint of both security and counterintelligence. It would prove the academic "intelligence cycle"—that starting with Essential Elements of Information (EEIs) and following the prescribed order of "direction, collection, interpretation, evaluation, collation, and dissemination," intelligence could lead to an effective command decision aimed at the ultimate goal of inflicting maximum damage upon the enemy. It would prove, too, that certain documents should not be carried into the field, or, if they were carried, should be destroyed if in danger of capture.

When the Third Army was forced to halt its offensive in September, the 17th SS also settled down, first northeast of Nancy and then in the threatened area across the Moselle southeast of Metz. But even then it was a moving outfit, difficult to pinpoint. Our broad EEIs had initially called for information on "location, identification, disposition, strength, and morale of the enemy" in our zone of advance. More recently, the location of command posts of our "favorites" had been specifically included, with "special emphasis on 17th SS Panzer Grenadier, 21st Panzer and 11th Panzer divisions."

At dusk on October 31, a reconnaissance patrol departed the 17th SS command post, proceeding by way of Metz to Jouy-Aux-Arches. There extremely heavy mortar fire forced the patrol's abandonment of its vehicle, and the patrol proceeded on foot to Corny. Stealthily crossing the Moselle by small boat, the group reached Arnaville before daybreak and hid there for the day. That night, November 1, it was captured at Bayonville.

A front-line search disclosed that the patrol, composed of two officers and one enlisted man from the 17th SS intelligence section, carried maps showing the precise location of their command post southwest of Peltre. The maps were taken intact.

Air photos, immediately requested and made, showed the town bustling with military activity. An immediate appeal was made through all intelligence collection agencies—including the OSS and FFI, the clandestine French force—for specific locations of the various headquarters buildings. Answers came soon. By November 6, the exact location of the division command post had been established, as had living quarters and offices of the division commander and his Ia (operations officer) and Ic (intelligence officer).

Of even greater importance from a tactical point of view, we had also pinpointed headquarters of the division signal battalion, the nerve center of its communications. Also located were two equally important targets of avoidance, a prisoner of war compound and a military hospital, both close by.

At mid-morning on November 8, a fighter-bomber squadron of the XIX TAC commenced a low-altitude, precision-bombing attack on the enemy installations at Peltre. Shortly after noon, TAC headquarters flashed the message, "Destroyed five buildings and several damaged in target area. Strafed and damaged six gun positions in target area...." The PW enclosure and hospital were untouched.

Later information confirmed the success of the attack. The bombing had wrought complete destruction. Early in December, advance elements of the Third Army passing through the town would see for themselves.

*****

From the day the Third Army became active on the Continent, the G-2 Section had encountered great difficulty in keeping enemy order of battle data posted in terms of accurate meaning. The Germans had thrown many divisions against the invasion, but because Allied air power prevented large road movements the latecomers among them were committed piecemeal. These units and the ones in the original assault area were soon to be considered destroyed as far as effective division combat strength was concerned. There were few division symbols left on the map which, in reality, represented effective combat divisions. Instead, most represented only remnants of divisions which had been badly mauled by Allied forces, or elements of divisions of which other units were yet to arrive.

By August 6, the Germans had committed a total of thirty-four divisions of all types against the Normandy invasion. These included a Panzer strength of ten divisions, which we usually kept separate on the books. The estimated total combat strength of the remaining twenty-four *at the time they were committed* was 237,000 men. We'd estimated losses at 137,800, however, leaving only 99,200 combat effectives to fight. The equivalent of eight divisions had been completely destroyed, and in terms of an average 10,000 men per division, only the equivalent of eleven divisions actually remained in combat. Yet, most of the twenty-four infantry divisions ever committed were still identifiable by small units still in combat on the field of battle. The ten Panzer divisions which had been committed had an estimated initial combat strength of 146,000 troops, but had suffered losses estimated at 59,500. Although ten divisions were still identified in contact, they had an actual equivalent strength of only five and a half divisions. They had an estimated total of 875 tanks of all types, considering that some heavy tank battalions had been attached.

As opposed to estimating the number of prisoners of war, the problem of estimating enemy killed or wounded was more involved—and not so easily verified. The Allies made provisions for their own anticipated casualties by providing hospital beds for so many patients on a percentage-of-strength basis. Grave registration personnel were apportioned by estimating the numbers of men anticipated to be killed in action or dying from other causes. It was known how many men were wounded by various types of enemy action and weapons, and how many of these were returned to duty. These same criteria, then, could logically be applied to the enemy.

If a column of enemy troops were strafed and the length and type of column were indicated, we could assess a percentage of casualties with reasonable accuracy—particularly if the effects of the strafing were observed. Similarly, if enemy troop concentrations were bombed, we could make some reasonable estimate of casualties. PW interrogation also threw some light on the situation, as did overrun areas where the enemy had buried his dead. The numbers of enemy wounded processed through Allied medical channels gave us some idea of that type of casualty. But even with these considerations, the estimate of the enemy's killed and wounded remained just that—an estimate. The enemy, too, evacuated his casualties to the rear for burial or medical care whenever possible.

By September 3, we'd estimated that fifty-four German divisions of all types had been committed against the Allied invaders. Estimated losses had cut the total strength of the thirty-nine non-Panzer divisions from 371,000 to 106,700 men. Eighteen infantry divisions were considered destroyed as divisions. The fifteen Panzer divisions which had been committed had lost an estimated 120,000 of their initial 198,000 men, leaving the equivalent of only five Panzer divisions with a total of 475 tanks of all types in combat.

It had early become apparent that some appropriate administrative procedure had to be devised to equate such figures; we needed some method which would show the true enemy strength at a glance. The adjustment was readily accomplished by reducing all divisions to terms of combat-effective infantry or tank *battalions,* a procedure which was initiated by the Third Army while we were still in England.

Allied pre-invasion estimates had concluded that the Germans could muster twenty-one and a half divisions against the Allied beachhead area—a total of 126 infantry and fourteen Panzer battalions. Because of their forced piecemeal commitments, although the divisions appeared on the map, by D-Day plus five the enemy had been able to throw into combat the equivalent of only eighty-two infantry and fourteen Panzer battalions. Allied strength, computed on the same basis as units went ashore, by that time totalled 108 infantry battalions and twenty-nine tank battalions.

Disregarding numbers of or identities of the divisions, the Allies, at a glance, had a clear superiority in numbers.

That more realistic comparison was of intense interest during the critical early days of the invasion and was kept posted on a special chart on the war room map. Used throughout the war by the Third Army in all of our estimates of enemy capabilities, the battalion breakdown was adopted in later months of the war by SHAFE and prescribed for use by all commands.

In the months following, when the numbers of German divisions in contact grew, the numbers of unit symbols identifying enemy elements again got out of proportion to the true enemy strength. Some divisions were composed entirely of draftees just mobilized, others of personnel otherwise unprepared or unfit for military service. Some divisions lacked normal components. But the division to which each of these units belonged was nevertheless identified as present, its symbol always shown on the maps. Although the G-2 work sheets were kept in terms of effective battalions to balance the misleading map symbols, the battalions were reconverted on a special chart into effective division-equivalent strength.

Although it all made sense to him, General Patton preferred the many symbols, without too much emphasis on the equivalents listed opposite. Comparing them one day, he said jokingly, "It would be ideal if we could have three sets of figures—a low one for the troops, a high one for the press, and the real one for me."

Enemy losses in Panzers, guns, and vehicles could be more factually judged than personnel losses. Those figures were based on actual claims from air or ground observation, and were particularly exact in a war of movement. An encircled or withdrawing enemy, under great pressure and faced with the possibility of being overrun, was forced to abandon his heavy equipment. Such losses could be counted on the battlefield. In static warfare, the problem was more difficult. German procedures called for retrieval of their disabled vehicles and materiel, which they usually accomplished with great efficiency. A piece seen disabled one day would be removed during the night, out of sight the next day.

Three "Ms"—men, materiel, and mobility—were the basic factors we applied in assessing a unit's overall combat efficiency. Men did the fighting, took and held the ground, controlled the weapons. Materiel—weapons and ammunition—were necessary to inflict casualties. Mobility was essential if troops were to be in the proper place at the proper time, properly equipped. Coupled with these were the less tangible attributes of leadership, the will to fight, physical condition, and know-how achieved through training and combat experience. But if any one of the three "Ms" were even partially denied the enemy, his combat efficiency was impaired.

A simple analogy. A tank needed a crew, firepower, and means of locomotion. Without a crew it could not serve its intended purpose, even though its weapons were serviceable and its supplies of ammunition and gasoline complete. Nor could it serve with full efficiency if one or more of its crew members became casualties, or if it were out of ammunition, or if its motor had been hit, or a track destroyed. Under many possible conditions it might not be entirely useless, but its combat effectiveness would be materially reduced. Instead of an asset it would become a liability.

If the usefulness of a sufficient number of individual tanks had been destroyed, the combat efficiency of their platoon would be affected. If enough platoons had been rendered partially ineffective, the company efficiency suffered—and so on up the line. It was a direct application of the old adage, "For want of a nail...."

If a unit's combat effectiveness and combat efficiency were affected through losses, so were its capabilities. We were directly and vitally concerned, then, not only in the number of prisoners of war taken and the number of enemy dead and wounded, but also in the number of larger guns, tanks, motor vehicles, and aircraft captured or destroyed. Such figures had to be kept in mind at all times—and often

in sight. If actual figures were not available, we had to substitute intelligence estimates.

*****

In December, 1944, the Third Army was preparing a drive through to the Rhine
from the general line of the Saar, roughly opposite Metz and Nancy, with Frankfurt
as the objective. The dense and once-formidable Siegfried Line lay across the direction of attack. Detailed information on the areas selected for penetration was
necessary, and all our efforts were beamed in that direction.

The XIX TAC had flown innumerable photographic missions. The air photos
were meticulously interpreted. And then came a windfall.

Through routine reading of an intelligence report disseminated by higher headquarters, we learned that a German officer captured in southern France had detailed
information on the Siegfried Line. He loved his country, but was convinced it had
lost the war. He feared that Hitler would not surrender and felt it was his duty to
help save whatever might be left of Germany by doing what he could to bring the
war to a speedy end. He had a personal, detailed knowledge of portions of the Line
through which Third Army troops would attack. Arrangements were made to have
him transferred.

Billeting him in Nancy as a "guest" of the Third Army G-2 Section, we soon
found he possessed an astonishing amount of information. His memory was fantas-
tic. He could pinpoint on the air photos the field fortifications and outline their
construction, densities, fields of fire, and the calibers and types of weapons they
had been designed to accommodate. He could indicate places where fortifications
were undetectable in air photos.

"At this point, although you can't see it in this photograph," he would report,
"is a machine gun nest. Its field of fire covers that 'Y' in the road. It can also fire
into that draw and cover that open ground."

How could he be so positive? Years before, he had helped to put them there.

These data, all carefully checked and verified, were placed on overprinted,
large-scale maps and prepared for distribution to all units which were scheduled to
have these pinpointed targets as their combat objectives. The German counteroffensive—the Battle of the Bulge—changed our mission, but the end product of the
German prisoner's cooperation was transferred to the Seventh Army and used as
originally intended—to its fullest advantage.

7

THE FOG OF WAR

On December 9, 1944, at Third Army headquarters in Nancy, there was a special briefing. The subject was a matter of great and growing concern to me, a concern involving the strategic reserves being husbanded by the Germans to the north. These forces, even though located outside the zone of advance of the scheduled Third Army offensive to the east, presented certain enemy capabilities which would, if used, affect our operations, at least indirectly.

Allied plans laid in early October for a direct assault on Germany had been followed through by the three army groups on the western front. By November's end, Montgomery's Twenty-first Army Group, fighting in the northern zone, had cleared the lower reaches of the Rhine and opened the vital port of Antwerp in preparation for enveloping the Ruhr basin from the north.

In the center, Bradley's Twelfth Army Group was heavily engaged in the Aachen area, having committed up to seventeen American divisions in that offensive, with a concentration at its height of ten divisions on a front of only twenty-four miles. Patton's Third Army had taken Metz and continued eastward to establish bridgeheads across the Moselle and engage the Siegfried Line. To the south, Lieutenant General Jacob L. Devers's Sixth Army Group had reached Belfort and the Rhine. All had slugged their way through the enemy, the terrain, and the weather, about equal in terms of opposition.

Then, early in December, the western banks of the Meuse had been cleared. The Roer had been reached. The Third Army crossed the German frontier and was well on its way to the Rhine. There would be no respite for the Germans, because a new Third Army offensive was in the making. Its objective was Frankfurt, by way of Kaiserslautern and the Palatinate. The jump-off date had been set for December 19, then changed to December 21.

On the nineteenth, headquarters would move from Nancy to St. Avold. By that time, communications would be installed, supply and ammunition dumps would be established well forward, terrain studies and detailed reports of enemy defensive positions long since would have been completed and distributed. Troops were already established in their jump-off areas. The Siegfried Line, under constant air photo scrutiny, had been studied and analyzed in minutest detail.

From the Allied viewpoint, Germany's continuation of the war had not made sense for some time. Hitler's armies had suffered a series of major defeats with disastrous losses. Twice they had nearly been encircled, at Falaise and at the Seine. The Mediterranean had been lost and Italy's mountain fastnesses were slowly but surely being reduced and conquered. All of France was lost. There remained only an ever-shrinking Germany—shrinking from west to east at a rate of about one hundred air-miles per month.

Why did Hitler keep going? Did he plan to hold the Siegfried Line at all costs? Was he trading space for time to develop a secret weapon to supplant the *Luftwaffe,* now practically inert? Would he go down before admitting to himself that he was wrong, taking his Germany with him?

Of greatest concern at the moment, however, was why, hardpressed as the German forces were, these troops were being held in reserve in the north. Strategic as well as tactical units had been reforming and refitting for months. They included, in formidable numbers, Panzers, Panzer Grenadiers, paratroops, and elite SS troops. Was Hitler holding them opposite the Aachen area, where the threat of Allied breakthrough was greatest, for a counterattack? Or were some of them there to spoil the planned offensive by the Third Army?

These were the questions under discussion at the special briefing at Patton's headquarters on December 9. G-2 Section concern, already great, was growing by the hour.

By the end of October, I pointed out, Panzer divisions had been reported reforming in the Paderborn area, just north of Frankfurt. Four had been identifed: the 130th Panzer Lehr, the 9th SS, 12th SS, and 2nd SS. We were receiving, fragmentarily, confirmation of their locations. One might well be the Panzer division now reported in the Düren area, another the one in the vicinity of Cologne, and a third that had recently moved into the Bielefeld area.

Large enemy ammunition and gasoline dumps had been reported, as had mines and unassembled enemy artillery pieces. All were pinpointed on the map. Air reconnaissance had reported at least one armored division with Panther and Tiger tanks on trains from Frankfurt going southwestward toward Merzig, and toward Saarbrücken. There had been constant reports of heavy loadings in the Paderborn area.

Five paratroop divisions, the 2nd, 3rd, 5th, 6th, and 7th, were reported to be in strategic reserve but we had not as yet located them. There were also reports that an 8th Paratroop Division was being formed. The 2nd Panzer Division had been reported in the Mönchen-Gladbach area on November 14, apparently having moved there since September 6.

There had also been reports that three infantry divisions, the 348th, the 326th, and the 243rd, were reforming in Westphalia.

By November 10 there had been a series of withdrawals of armor. The 11th Panzer Division had been last contacted by XII Corps of Third Army on October 25, the 9th Panzer by the Twenty-First Army Group on October 31. The 2nd SS Panzer Division was last contacted by First Army's VIII Corps on November 2. The 2nd Panzer Division had also withdrawn from its front, contacted last on November 3, when it was learned that its main body had moved to Westphalia during the period of October 21-22. The 21st Panzer Division had last been contacted to the south by Seventh Army on November 7.

Of fifteen Panzer divisions then listed in the West, only five remained in contact with Allied forces. Two definitely were out of recent contact, five were reforming, and three others were in a questionable status as only partial elements had been observed.

A heavy schedule of night photo reconnaissance missions had been requested, with particular emphasis on railroad marshalling yards and important highway intersections deep within Germany. Actual performance was sometimes hard to come by, our requested missions deviating somewhat from normal practices. By arrangement, however, the XIX Tactical Air Command was permitted to fly in areas directly in front of the First Army because its reconnaissance group was in a location which permitted more extensive flying than that of the First Army's IX TAC.

Photo interpreters had been able to trace the progress of several hundred railroad trains photographed on daily missions. They were able to estimate the size of units being transferred, and later to estimate the large buildup of German divisions by counting the empty cars on sidings. So detailed were their findings that, had it been useful, they could have reproduced operating schedules of those portions of the German railroad system under their surveillance.

On November 17, huge enemy rail movements had been uncovered. More than three hundred train sections and locomotives were observed east and west of the

Rhine. The marshalling yards of the area were extremely active, with many military train sections in evidence. The vast majority of movement observed was found to be to the southwest and west, into the Third Army zone of advance.

Increased rail activity also was in evidence on November 18 and 19. On the eighteenth, 226 trains were reported operating in Third Army's projected zone. At the same time, a great number of stationary trains were noted in the marshalling yards on the west and south rail routes. Numerous trains entering the Third Army area were made up of flatcars loaded with armor and motor vehicles. Higher headquarters reported that a Panzer division and possibly an infantry division were being moved to the Third Army front.

On November 21, a prisoner of war had told of seeing a secret order that all qualified English-speaking personnel were to be sent to Osnabrück for training in reconnaissance, sabotage, and espionage, and that all captured Allied uniforms would be sent to that place.

By November 23, the five reconstituted Panzer divisions of the then-identified Sixth Panzer Army, along with the six reformed paratroop divisions of the First Paratroop Army, had continued to constitute a formidable strategic reserve "for either piecemeal or coordinated counteroffensive employment."* Considering three divisions in Scandinavia and the constantly expanding Volks Grenadier divisions in Germany, the enemy could, we estimated, have another eight infantry divisions capable of commitment in the West by December 1.

The 130th Panzer Lehr Division had been identified in contact and definitely fixed as a unit of the Sixth Panzer Army under command of Colonel General Sepp Dietrich. This led us to deduce that the Sixth Panzer Army might have served as an administrative headquarters controlling the reformation of all the Panzer divisions in the Paderborn area. With the 130th identified, it might well be that other elements of that Panzer army might also begin to appear, with any of its remaining four divisions as candidates.

On November 26, the air reconnaissances had again reported considerable rail activity. Sufficient observation of rail movement had been made to warrant the estimate that another division was being committed to bolster the enemy defenses. Thirty-three trains were reported moving in a southwesterly direction, and three days later the German 245th Infantry Division was identified in front of the United States Seventh Army to the south.

As I had outlined the situation on November 30, the enemy had six Panzer divisions, at least four paratroop divisions, and at least four infantry divisions out

* *Third Army G-2 Periodic Report #165.*

of the line. In addition, four reformed Volks Grenadier divisions were estimated ready for commitment. *

Three divisions from outside the immediate theater (those in Scandinavia) had been reported as having left for the West. No divisions from the Italian front had appeared in the West since August, but if the enemy there shortened his lines before the winter snows set in, some four or five additional divisions might be released for employment on the western front.

On December 2, the Seventh Army had reported the 130th Panzer Lehr out of contact on its XV Corps front. Some infantry divisions were reported going in, others going out.

As of December 7, with the enemy holding a combined total of thirteen divisions in reserve, our *Third Army G-2 Periodic Report* had pointed out that the most important factor regarding those reserves continued to be the large Panzer concentration west of the Rhine. Located in the northern portion of the Twelfth Army Group's zone of advance, this concentration then contained at least three of the four SS Panzer divisions previously estimated, the 1st SS, 2nd SS, and the 9th SS. Of the remainder, the 116th Panzer Division was undergoing reformation east of the Rhine, and the 12th SS and 2nd Panzer divisions had been recently reported moving south toward the Third Army zone.

The need for infantry units on the fighting front had been growing increasingly acute, so much so that the enemy had been forced to commit some of his reformed paratroop divisions. The 5th and 8th Paratroop divisions still were held in reserve, however.

Trains with flatcars possibly loaded with armor or motor transport had continued to be reported entering the Third Army zone, portraying the probability of a buildup of enemy troops and supplies mostly north of, but astride the Moselle River directly opposite the boundary between the First Army's VIII Corps and Third Army's XX Corps. It was the continued movement toward the Third Army zone which now brought the matter to a head.

By December 9, the situation north of the Moselle demanded special attention. The principle that the purpose of intelligence is to assist the commander in accomplishing his mission and to protect the command from surprise was plainly applicable. What if the enemy attacked to the west, just north of the Moselle? It would certainly have some effect on the operations of Third Army, heading east as it would be in a matter of ten days. Although out of our zone of advance, it would be a threat to our flank.

* Respectively, the 1st SS, 2nd SS, 9th SS, 12th SS, 2nd, and 116th Panzers; the 2nd, 5th, 7th, and 8th Paratroop; the 85th, 331st, 363rd, and 719th Infantry; and the 49th, 276th, 326th, and 352nd Volks Grenadiers.

A point is stressed here, not defensively. Enemy *strategic* reserves are accounted for by headquarters with strategic intelligence interests. Too much over-expansion of subordinate headquarters' interest is viewed askance in intelligence circles. The minimum of people must know what is going on in the clandestine intelligence collection field, the responsibility of highest echelons. A little knowledge may be dangerous, too much may negate the entire effort. We were minding our own business when we overlapped the armies to the north and south in sufficient depth, intelligence-wise, to protect our flanks. We would have no right, implied or expressed, to roam the enemy rear areas indiscriminately to see what was going on. That was not a tactical headquarters responsibility.

We had no reason to challenge either the competence or quality of the intelligence received from other quarters. The analysis and interpretation of such intelligence, however, was the function and responsibility of each G-2 as it applied to his commander's mission. Abundant information was at hand to support the deductions we made and the views expressed in the Patton headquarters from the time of the December 9 briefing at Nancy. History was to prove them entirely correct.

Confined principally to the threat opposite the VIII Corps—a threat on the northern flank of the projected Third Army offensive—the enemy capabilities were presented to the small group in Patton's headquarters that day as they were then seen through the eyes of our G-2 Section. All of the details on which the capability estimates were based had been documented in our official reports; it was the composite of what those details might mean which was new.

The Germans had four infantry divisions in contact with the VIII Corps. In addition there were two Panzer divisions with an estimated 105 tanks in immediate reserve, and three Volks Grenadier divisions in strategic reserve.* Of the nine numbered divisions now opposite the VIII Corps (with its three divisions on the line and one armored division in reserve on a front of some eighty miles extending to the north from Trier), the enemy combat equivalent strength was estimated as a total of seven German divisions, five and a half infantry and one and a half Panzer. This, it was pointed out at the December 9 briefing, was of considerable significance.

In front of the VIII Corps, I told Patton and other members of the Third Army command staff, stood two and a half more enemy divisions in equivalent strength than against the entire Third Army, three and a half divisions more than against the entire Seventh Army, and only one division less than the equivalent strength of all

---

* Respectively, the 18th, 26th, and 212th Volks Grenadier and the 352nd Infantry divisions; the 2nd Panzer and 130th Panzer Lehr divisions, and the 560th—recently arrived from Denmark—62nd, and 362nd Volks Grenadier divisions.

of the enemy divisions then in contact on the First Army front (of which the VIII Corps was a component).

The location of the two Panzer divisions in immediate tactical reserve and the three Volks Grenadier divisions in strategic reserve, I noted, gave the enemy a number of capabilities: He could meet threats in either the First or Third Army zones of advance by shuttling his forces north or south; he could, by causing sufficient apprehension, divert Allied reinforcements needed for the battle line to meet his possible threat in that area, or he could use that reserve to launch a spoiling or diversionary offensive.

In discussion it was pointed out that in a possible counteroffensive the enemy was favored by certain additional factors: He now had a rested and refitted fighter air force capable of putting one thousand planes into the air for a short period of time; his five rested and refitted divisions in reserve (with four other divisions in contact) were in a sector which had been relatively quiet for several months, and the terrain, although uninviting for winter campaigning by the Allies, was favorable to enemy offensive operations.

A brief terrain estimate also was given. Comparable to that in the northern portion of the Third Army's XX Corps zone, the terrain was rolling and open, generally favorable to cross-country movement. No major stream or ridge system dissected the area. It had an abundance of good cover and concealment. There were no known organized lines of defensive positions.

The friendly strength also was reviewed. In addition to the VIII Corps' four assigned divisions, an additional armored division (the 10th) was undergoing rest and refitting southeast of Luxembourg in the Third Army zone. This would make three United States infantry and two United States armored divisions available for immediate employment in the general area.

In conclusion, I explained, the enemy had an approximate two-to-one numerical advantage in the area, offset to some extent by low combat efficiency of poorly trained and inexperienced units. His buildup had been gradual and highly secret. A successful diversionary attack, even of a limited nature, would have a great psychological effect—a "shot in the arm" for Germany and Japan.

The briefing was followed by a short silence. Nothing, it was then agreed, would interfere with the plans already underway for the Third Army drive on Frankfurt. Limited outline planning would begin at once to meet the threat to the north, however, both to play it safe and to be readily available for use if needed.

General Patton arose.

"We'll be in a position to meet whatever happens," he told the group.

The plans so begun would be used, in a big way, before the month was over.

In the days following, messages and reports continued to pour in. German divisions were moving in and out of contact. The *Third Army Weekly G2 Report* of December 11 noted that, with the Allied winter offensive grinding into its second month and the Germans losing an estimated three divisions a week, certain significant facts stood out in the West.

"Despite the drain of large losses," it said, "the enemy continued to maintain a cohesive line along the entire front without drawing heavily on his Panzer reserves. During the week, the enemy actually withdrew two Panzer divisions from contact and although committing the 719th Infantry Division against the Third United States Army, his only major reinforcement in the West during the week, the enemy continued to hold the bulk of his infantry reserve out of the line."

The report further noted that despite continued heavy losses in men and equipment, the enemy, powerfully aided by the weather and his prepared defensive positions, was able without apparent undue difficulty to maintain a well controlled "defend and delay" struggle along the entire front. We considered it significant that this defense had been conducted with a minimum of armor.

By the end of the week, only six Panzer-type divisions were definitely in contact. Two of these were in the North against the Ninth Army and Montgomery's Twenty-First Army Group, the other four in the South opposing the Third and Seventh Armies.* During the week, the badly battered 130th Panzer Lehr was withdrawn from the XII-XV Corps fronts and the equally mauled 10th SS Panzer Division left the Ninth Army and Twenty-First Army Group zone. The 3rd Panzer Grenadier Division had not been contacted for several days on either the First or Ninth Army fronts, and it too might well have been withdrawn from the line.

"Thus," the *G-2 Weekly Report* continued, "excluding the 3rd Panzer Grenadier Division as of this date, the enemy has eight Panzer Divisions* out of the line, with the strong possibility that the 5th SS Panzer Division may have come to the West, making a total of nine Panzers in reserve....Overall, the initiative still rests with the Allies, but the massive armored force the enemy has built up in reserve gives him the definite capability of launching a spoiling (diversionary) offensive to disrupt the Allied drive.

"On the basis of the above enumerated significant facts, it is indicated that although the Allied offensive is destroying weekly a number of German divisions, nevertheless the enemy has been able to maintain a cohesive front, without drawing on the bulk of his infantry and armor reserves, thereby giving him the capability of

---

* Respectively the 9th, 11th, and 21st Panzer and 15th, 25th, and 17th SS Panzer Grenadier divisions. The 9th Panzer and 15th Panzer Grenadier were in the North, the 11th Panzer, 21st Panzer, and 25th and 17th SS Panzer Grenadier divisions in the South.

mounting a spoiling offensive in an effort to unhinge the Allied assault on *Festung Deutschland....* "

On December 13, a high-ranking prisoner of war reported he had been told sometime in August that it was impossible to supply the divisions engaged on the western front with fresh troops. All men who could be spared from the Navy, *Luftwaffe,* etc., would be required to join Volks Grenadier divisions. These divisions were to form an assault army under the command of Colonel General Sepp Dietrich. About seventy Volks Grenadier divisions were then the objective, he said, ten of them to be used as "blocking" divisions for stopping the Allies short of German borders. The remaining "assault" divisions were to be used for a single large-scale counterattack on the western front, scheduled for the end of December.

The prisoner went on to say that the German high command had hopes of achieving a large-scale breakthrough, based on its intelligence estimates that the Allied positions in France were not constructed in depth, that the Allies had no reserve divisions behind the actual fighting lines, and that the American soldier was war-weary.

Our *G-2 Periodic Report* of December 14 continued to detail the evidence of an enemy buildup. Despite the growing need for reinforcement in the areas of Allied advance, the Germans persisted in holding key armored divisions in reserve. "It is evident from the determined hoarding of Sixth SS Panzer Army units that the enemy is making every effort to employ this armor in a coordinated effort," we noted. "He is already bending over backward to avoid piecemeal commitment."

On December 15 the G-2 report quoted a prisoner taken in the XII Corps zone who claimed to have heard Hitler "give a talk recently that troops should hold because in two weeks a German counteroffensive would be launched." Also, "A PW from the 17th SS Panzer Grenadier captured the night of December 13-14 stated that he was carrying a verbal message which, recorded and translated was, 'Last night's message ordering your retreat was false. Everyone is to hold and prepare for a counterattack that is in the making.'"

On December 16, the *Third Army G-2 Periodic Report,* covering the period ending the previous midnight, stated three significant indications under strategic order of battle notes headed "Reforming Armored Reserve":

"(1) In Sixth Panzer Army area east of the Roer River and west of the Rhine, between Düsseldorf and Cologne, 1st SS, 2nd SS, 9th SS, 12th SS, 10th SS, and 116th Panzer Divisions appear to be reforming.

---

* The 1st SS, 2nd SS, 9th SS, 10th SS, 12th SS, 2nd, 116th, and 130th Panzer divisions.

"(2) In the area of Trier, Kyllburg, Wittlich, 2nd Panzer and 130th Panzer Lehr Divisions appear to be reforming with 116th Panzer Division reported slated for that area.

"(3) Just out of the line and in positions of tactical mobile reserve 9th Panzer Division (Ninth United States Army Zone) and 3rd Panzer Grenadier Division (VII United States Corps Zone) appear to be reforming.

"From these indications it appears that:

"(1) The enemy is reforming and refitting his battered Panzer divisions but at the same time is keeping them available for immediate employment in the event of a serious threat of a major breakthrough.

"(2) The enemy is massing his armor in positions of tactical reserve presumably for a large-scale counteroffensive."

Patton's Third Army was watching, but not waiting. Our own eastward offensive would be launched on schedule on December 21.

8

GERMAN PRELUDE TO THE BULGE

The study of German military records after the war showed that data on which notes for the special December 9 briefing in Nancy had been based was remarkably accurate. The four German divisions we listed in contact opposite the VIII Corps (the 18th Volks Grenadier, 26th Volks Grenadier, 212th Volks Grenadier, and 352nd Infantry) were actually present on the ground. We had also identified correctly the two armored divisions in immediate reserve. The 2nd Panzer Division had assembled in the Bitburg-Wittlich area during the month of November, while the 130th Panzer Lehr Division had moved into the same area from Saarbrücken in thirty-two trains, commencing on December 8. Its last units arrived on December 16.

The strategic reserve we listed at the briefing included the 560th Volks Grenadier Division from Denmark and the 62nd and 362nd Volks Grenadier divisions from Germany. The 560th left Denmark in thirty trains, starting December 4, destined for the Kyllburg area. Its last unit arrived there December 18. The 62nd moved from Neuhammer to the Wittlich area during the period November 28-December 3. It was then assembled north of Prüm on December 9. Our listing of the 362nd was an error, though apparently a simple transposition of numbers. The 326th Volks Grenadier Division departed Pressburg, Slovakia, in thirty-eight trains starting November 26 and detraining in part opposite the VIII Corps in the Kyllburg area on December 5. It was assembled as a division southeast of Monschau toward the north central part of the area, starting December 9.

The Germans knew Allied strengths and weaknesses well. Their intelligence maps of December 7 were remarkably accurate as to the Allied troop dispositions. On the Allied front from the United States XIX and VII Corps boundary south to the Colmar Pocket, they had missed on only two divisions. They carried the 7th Armored Division in VII Corps reserve, whereas it actually was committed north of the 104th Infantry Division. They also had failed to identify the 9th Armored Division in the VIII Corps sector. They had placed correctly the boundary between the XIX and VII Corps, although they had shown it with a question mark. No boundaries were shown between the United States V and VII Corps nor between the V and VIII Corps. They had placed the boundary between the First and Third armies too far north, and no boundary was shown between the Third Army's XX and XII Corps. The line they showed between the Twelfth and Sixth Army Groups was approximately correct.

Placed side by side, a German operations map and our G-2, G-3 map for December 7 were practically identical concerning opposing units in contact and in immediate reserve.

The German operations map was a mass of "goose eggs"— ellipsoidal symbols indicating assembly areas for their troops actually present. Arrows with explanatory remarks indicated troop movements into various areas, generally opposite the United States VIII Corps. The movements were to be made at night, under cover of darkness, according to a carefully laid out plan.

The general area of German troop concentration was bounded on the south by the Moselle River from Trier to Koblenz, then north along the Rhine through Bonn and Cologne to Düsseldorf, then west to Roermond.

The front lines, passing through the Aachen area southward, completed the area boundaries on the west. All told, the buildup area covered some 4,500 square miles, averaging about fifty air miles east to west and ninety miles north to south.

The German map showed an open-ended "goose egg" marking the area which the 5th Paratroop Division would occupy once it was assembled opposite the United States VIII Corps. The 5th Paratroop was at that time en route to the area from Amsterdam and Rotterdam. The first of its forty-one trains, it was noted, already had cleared Koblenz. The division was to be assembled in the assigned area during the night of December 13-14.

The map also showed a miscellany of other units and their assembly areas, including those to be held in reserve west of the Rhine. A total of 136 troop trains were that very day bringing German forces into the buildup area, sixty-five of them in the southern third of the area, north of the Moselle—opposite the United States VIII Corps.

The German *Feindlage* (enemy situation) maps of higher headquarters showed Allied front lines by a black line of varying width. The width of the line depended on the density of Allied troops at that point. In a part of the front where they were opposed by heavy troop concentration, the line would be relatively wide; where lightly held by the enemy, it would be relatively narrow. The line on their map of December 7, titled "Enemy Situation in the West," was very wide up north in the Aachen area. It was also comparatively wide in the area south of the Moselle. But in the Ardennes, lightly held by the American VIII Corps, the front was represented by a mere hairline.

*****

The initial German plan for the Ardennes counteroffensive, in the form of a written directive approved by *Generaloberst* Alfred Jodl, was dated November 1, 1944. According to records now in the military archives, the basic German thinking about an offensive in the Ardennes started toward the end of September. The higher commanders, Field Marshal Karl Rudolph Gerd von Rundstedt and Field Marshal Walther Model, were briefed in person by Hitler on or about October 28. The written directive, titled "Basic Planning for the Operation *'Wacht am Rhein',*" stated briefly that the object of the planned operation was destruction of the enemy to the north of the general Antwerp-Brussels-Bastogne line.

The directive charged Model's Army Group B (with the Sixth SS Panzer Army on the north, Fifth Panzer Army in the center, and the Seventh Army on the south) with following short artillery shellings with a breakthrough in a number of tactically favorable localities. The Sixth SS Panzer Army would rapidly seize the Meuse crossings on either side of Liege, gaining them intact in cooperation with "Operation Skorzeny."

SS *Obersturmbannführer* Otto Skorzeny had been briefed on the latter by Hitler on October 22, ahead of the high command. To take the Meuse bridges intact, Hitler had called for the use of a clandestine force using Allied uniforms, vehicles, and equipment. To be called the 150th Panzer Brigade, it would consist of one Panzer company, three Panzer reconnaissance companies, and two motorized infantry battalions. Anti-air, antitank, artillery, and signal detachments would be organized into platoons. The entire force would number about 2,700 men.

Commando detachments in small groups of five or six men would be trained in demolitions to destroy bridges, gasoline and ammunition dumps. Other detachments of three or four men would form reconnaissance and signal patrols. Radio-equipped, they would, in addition to their reconnaissance missions, transmit false orders, change direction signs, remove minefield markers, and do anything else they could to create confusion for Allied troops.

Skorzeny's mission was top secret, but it could not be kept so for long. With the recruiting of personnel, rumors started. The Germans couldn't stop them so they used them to their own advantage by enlarging upon them. The rumors worked well. "Skorzeny" soon became a feared and respected name among the Allies.*

The Sixth SS Panzer Army would, according to the German plan, subsequently build up strong defensive positions facing north along the Vesdre River and man the eastern fortifications of Liege. It also would take the Albert Canal between Maastricht and Antwerp and then operate in the area to the north of Antwerp.

The Fifth Panzer Army, meanwhile, would use the principal highway to Bastogne and cross the Meuse between Amay and Namur and prevent Allied reserve operations against the rear of the Sixth SS Panzer Army along the Antwerp-Brussels-Namur-Dinant line.

The German Seventh Army, operating to the south of the army group, would protect the flank to the south and southwest. Its initial objective would be to reach the Meuse and the Semois rivers and establish contact with the Moselle front in the area east of Luxembourg. It would take as much ground as possible, gaining time by use of demolitions and then building up a solid defensive position toward its rear. Its mission would be mainly defensive, being reinforced with additional engineer units and numerous anti-tank units.

The breakthrough of Army Group B would be exploited by Army Group H in the north as soon as the Allies reacted. It would attack either toward the area between the Ruhr and Meuse rivers or against the Albert Canal. This secondary attack would be pressed, according to the situation as it developed, either eastwards of the Juliana Canal toward the south or through the Venlo bridgehead toward the west or southwest.

Beginning immediately, the November 1 directive ordered, individual divisions would be prepared for their future missions. To assure the secrecy of the buildup, the plan was accompanied by orders covering security which provided the death penalty for those who failed to live up to prescribed restrictions.

Following the general concept of the German plan as first announced, Army Group B gave its northern Fifteenth Army a frontage extending southward about fifty miles from a Roermond-Düsseldorf line. It would comprise three corps, with a total of ten infantry divisions on the line. Eight of these would have been committed prior to the time of the assault. It would have in tactical reserve one infantry

---

* The taking of the bridges by Skorzeny's force failed to materialize when the Ardennes counteroffensive actually came. The gap through which his Panzer brigade was to pass on the morning of the attack, December 16, did not provide enough room for rapid movement. His front was simply too narrow.

division, two Panzer Grenadier divisions, and one Panzer division. Two of these reserve divisions were in the southern part of its zone, just north of the Fifteenth Army boundary which would lie along the line Eupen to Euskirchen.

The Sixth SS Panzer Army's two corps would initially have a front of about twenty-five miles. It would have seven divisions on the line for the assault—four Volks Grenadier divisions, one paratroop division, and two Panzer divisions. Three of these would have been in contact before the actual time of jump-off. Back-up would be provided by the II SS Panzer Corps consisting of two SS Panzer divisions, the 2nd and the 9th. The army's southern boundary would be an east-west line lying just to the north of St. Vith.

The Fifth Panzer Army with three corps would have a front of about twenty-five miles. It would consist of seven divisions for the assault, four of them Volks Grenadier and the other three Panzers. Only two of them would appear before the jump-off. Its southern boundary would pass through Bastogne.

The Seventh Army, with three corps, would be the southernmost of Army Group B, on a front of about thirty miles. Two of its corps with two divisions each would be just north of the Moselle. The other would consist of static groups. Of its four divisions, only two would have been in contact just prior to the assault. Three divisions would be Volks Grenadier, the other paratroop. The Seventh Army's southern boundary (and that of the army group) would be a general line extending east-west through Trier.

The scheduled array of German military force to be ready at the time of the counteroffensive's kick-off on December 16 was a formidable one. It totaled twenty-eight divisions from north to south, plus six divisions in tactical reserve to be pushed through immediately, and another division in army group reserve. Eight divisions were to be in strategic reserve (and so beyond the control of the army group commander). In all, the commitment would total forty-three divisions.

The Germans recognized that to mass these troops without arousing suspicions of an impending counterattack obviously would be a difficult task. Strict security would prevail. The troop dispositions would be explained as precautionary steps in preparation for an expected Allied breakthrough in the Aachen area. All dispositions were purely defensive in nature. Even the operation's code name, highly classified, would have that connotation—"The Watch on the Rhine." Nothing so much as suggested any aggressive action on the part of the German forces.

To preserve secrecy to the last minute, even so common a term as "D-Day" was done away with. Instead, they used an alphabetical arrangement. A certain day was to be known as "K-Day," followed by "L," "M," "N," and "O." "O-Day" would be December 16, the date set for the attack.

Phase lines behind which troops would be assembled in terms of the lettered days were drawn up. These were spaced about ten kilometers (about six miles) apart. Infantry troops would be brought up to within ten kilometers of the front by marching, to arrive at the final phase line twenty-four hours before the assault. On the night that infantry troops were to reach that line, the tracked vehicles were to be brought up to within fifteen kilometers of the front. Then, all units which would constitute the first assault wave would be brought up to their attack positions during the darkness of the night of December 15-16. There were to be no contacts with the enemy until the attack was launched.

The stage was set for what would go down in history as the Ardennes counter-offensive, the Battle of the Bulge.

9

THE FOG LIFTS

December 16 started the way most of the recent days had, "mostly cloudly to overcast this morning, becoming mostly cloudly in afternoon and mostly cloudly to overcast near the end of the forecast period. Occasional light drizzle and rain during the morning. Visibility poor in light fog, improving somewhat during the afternoon. Light southwesterly surface winds entire period. Temperature reaching low 40s this afternoon...." And the coming night, the forecast said, would be "mostly cloudly to overcast with light intermittent rain near end of period. Visibility restricted...temperature in the high 30s."

The weather that had plagued the troops and kept Allied air power idle—the rains, the mists, the fog of varying intensities, and the resulting limited visibility— would continue.

But on this day another fog—the fog of war—would start to lift.

Reports were filtering in. Up north, the First Army's VII Corps advance continued, hotly and bitterly disputed by determined enemy troops. Enemy counterattacks were launched. In the V Corps zone, mines, wire, and constant artillery fire slowed the advance considerably.

There was a report of two "unidentified" individuals dressed as United States Army officers who had visited an American anti-aircraft installation asking many questions about AA defenses, the communications setup, and front line locations in the First Army zone. They said they had been near the Roer River, but apparently had no transportation of their own. One was a captain, wearing a .45 caliber pistol, the other a first lieutenant armed with a carbine; both were wearing olive drab clothes with new trench coats. Another report told of a PW taken in the northern portion of the VIII Corps area earlier in the day. The prisoner said he had helped lay wire in that area for the 1st SS Panzer Division during the past three days.

Elements recognized as part of the Sixth SS Panzer Army were identified in contact. Armed air reconnaissance encountered intense and accurate flak opposite the VIII Corps at 3:40 P.M., possibly indicating the presence of a new division in the area. Heavy enemy vehicle and rail traffic was stopped twelve miles northeast of Trier at 1:00 P.M. headed south. At 10:45 P.M., the XIX Tactical Air Command night fighters reported two convoys, each approximately ten miles long, moving south and west toward the Hamburg-Neunkirchen area west of Saarbrücken. Explosions resulting when the vehicles were attacked indicated they were carrying ammunition or gasoline.

By midnight, it appeared that the enemy had launched attacks along the entire VIII Corps front and the southern portion of the VII Corps front, immediately to its north. The majority of the reported attacks were near the center of the VIII Corps zone, and had already resulted in limited penetration. A total of seven new divisions—three Panzer and four infantry—were identified in the VIII Corps zone during the day.

Enemy paratroops had been dropped in rear areas, reports indicated, in groups of fifteen to twenty, without concerted efforts to attack. It was suspected that their mission was sabotage and guerrilla activity.

In Third Army headquarters, we watched these developments with intense interest and concern. An early report from the Twelfth Army Group headquarters concluded that the enemy attacks might be a "powerful diversion to force the hurried withdrawal of our divisions from the vital Cologne and Saar River areas to meet the Eifel threat." But we saw the situation differently. In light of the identification of elements of the Sixth SS Panzer Army on the VIII Corps front, we stated in our Third Army intelligence reports, "it may well be that this is the enemy's major effort." Time alone would tell whether the attack was in fact more than a limited counterattack, whether it was the major effort, or whether another attack as the main effort would be made against the northern part of the Third Army zone where terrain was more favorable.

The soupy weather would be no help. For Monday, December 18, the forecast predicted a general overcast with light intermittent rains. Visibility would be three to five miles, lowering to one to two miles in precipitation. For the nineteenth and twentieth: "Mostly cloudly with overcast with showers of rain and snow. Good visibility lowering slightly in showers." For the twenty-first: "Partly overcast with intermittent rain. Moderate visibility." Temperatures would be in the 30s. The enemy would be virtually immune from the probing eyes of Allied aerial reconnaissance.

On the Third Army front, then facing east, the enemy attitude had continued during the day to be defensive and delaying in nature. We estimated that the enemy was capable of concentrating, within forty-eight hours, the equivalent of two infantry and one Panzer division in the Merzig-Trier area to launch a diversionary attack and relieve pressure against the Siegfried Line. And, in addition, within the same forty-eight hours the equivalent of one infantry and one Panzer division could be concentrated in the Zweibrücken-Pirmasens area, for the same purpose.

Those capabilities, indicated by the tactical situation in the VIII Corps front, were supported by Tactical Air Command reports of significant heavy rail and motor movement opposite the Third Army's southernmost XII Corps and the Seventh Army's northernmost XV Corps zones as well. These capabilities would remain of concern until the enemy activities in the First Army and Third Army zones became more clear. It was still the "Ace-in-the-hole" Sixth SS Panzer Army which bore most careful watching.

As of noon on December 17, the front lines of the VIII Corps could no longer be established. The enemy was gaining ground. German paratroops taken prisoner said their orders were to hold out for two days, by which time their positions were to be overrun by ground troops. They said their mission was to attack and control crossroads at important locations to prevent movement of Allied reinforcements and to disrupt communications. It was estimated that 350 to 400 paratroops had been dropped. More could be expected during the night of December 17-18.

The situation grew worse. Monschau fell to the enemy. In the VIII Corps zone, troops to the east in the Schnee Eifel area had been cut off. Sizeable penetrations had been made by the Germans. Reports were terse and dramatic: "Enemy elements reached...tanks and infantry pushed back...overrunning several Corps artillery batteries...Echternach still surrounded by enemy with fighting going on in nearby villages." The enemy action was aided and abetted by its air force, which had come out in strength in support of the ground operations, attacking ground troops and aggressively challenging Allied planes in aerial combat.

German prisoners said attacks were planned against the northern portion of the Third Army XX Corps zone. These reports, corroborated by Tactical Air Command reports of continuing movements by rail and road in the vicinity of Trier, indicated possible reinforcements coming into that area. Again, a Panzer division was a likely candidate. A definite increase of enemy activity in the area was reported: aggressive patrolling, increased artillery fire, and evidence of determined and accurate artillery adjustments. To the south of the XX Corps, the enemy attitude remained defensive.

By the night of December 18, five Panzer divisions had definitely been committed in the First Army zone. Seven new infantry divisions had been identified in the first thirty-six hours of the enemy drive. The enemy had committed the bulk of his Panzer and infantry reserves on the Eifel front.

The fog of war had lifted. Our Third Army intelligence reports concluded: "The enemy offensive is designed to disrupt the Allied winter drive to smash German military forces in the West; the enemy has committed the bulk of his Panzer and infantry reserves in the West, but still has available a group of divisions to exploit the gains made in the Eifel area; the Third and Seventh Armies' threat to the Siegfried Line continues an undiminished danger to the enemy which he may attempt to dissipate by making a thrust in the north sector of the United States XX Corps zone."

The enemy still had in reserve on that date three SS Panzer divisions, two paratroop divisions, and three infantry divisions.

The German penetration reached such proportion—forty miles in depth and thirty miles in width—that the command of VIII Corps troops south of the breakthrough was passed from the First to the Third Army. The Third Army then had a new mission, fighting now in two directions. A ninety-degree change of direction was necessary for its main effort to the north, while its older mission to the east on the Saar would continue. A part of its old southern front was taken over by the Seventh Army through a shift of the inter-army boundary to the north. The Third Army would "change direction and attack from the area Luxembourg-Arlon to destroy the enemy on its front and be prepared to change direction to the northeast and seize crossings of the Rhine River." These were the orders, effective at 1:30 P.M. on December 20.

On the eighteenth, at the direction of General Bradley, Patton was directed to proceed immediately from Nancy to Luxembourg to get the "feel" of the situation at Twelfth Army Group Headquarters and be prepared to establish what would, on the twentieth, become the headquarters of the "Mobile Command Group" of Third Army. Two other members of his command staff and I accompanied Patton.

The maps on hand were those carried in an open jeep. Communication was difficult. The intelligence staff back at Nancy headquarters continued to receive all of the reports, which were briefed and relayed to us or sent by courier, depending on their urgency. The officer couriers used were held long enough to act as liaison officers with the Twelfth Army Group G-2 Section as well.

The Third Army intelligence section was now split into two fully operational groups, both operating on a twenty-four hour basis, separated by ninety miles of hazardous, overcrowded roads. Publication and dissemination of the intelligence summaries and *G-2 Periodic Reports* continued at Nancy. For the next two days, the Nancy contingent also had primary responsibility for the southern front, the Luxembourg contingent for the Ardennes.

On December 22, with the exception of a few staff members left behind to do the full-scale briefings in the war room (which remained in Nancy until the twenty-eighth), the G-2 Section was rejoined in Luxembourg. There it functioned normally in spite of the extremely limited wartime appointments and facilities available in the technical high school building which served as temporary headquarters.

On December 18, the situation in the VIII Corps area was fluid. The general shape of the Bulge was established across northern Luxembourg and well into Belgium on the St. Vith-St. Hubert axis, its southern flank resting on the Echternach-Diekirch-Ettelbruck line and its northern flank on a line through Monschau, Malmedy, Stavelot, and Marche-en-Famenne. In the center lay Wiltz and Bastogne, the former already encircled.

The enemy had again received strong support from its air force and additional paratroops had been dropped.

An order taken from the body of a German officer of the 116th Panzer Division was spot disseminated by the First Army. The order, it stated, was to be distributed only shortly before the beginning of the attack. It covered Skorzeny's "Vulture" operation. That operation, according to the document, would be performed by German forces with American equipment, American weapons, American vehicles, and American insignia, with the Allies' five-pointed yellow or white star painted on their vehicles. To avoid confusion with Allied troops, the bogus troops would identify themselves during the day by taking off their steel helmets and at night by red-blue flashlight signals. Their locations and routes would be shown by white dots painted on houses and trees. Route plans were included. Distribution of written orders was forbidden.

General Hasso von Manteuffel, the commander, had added remarks admonishing all concerned that if vehicle difficulties developed—whether among the infantry, armored infantry, reconnaissance, or engineers—they would proceed on foot to their objectives.

Command briefings covering the new situation and the new Third Army area took place in the newly-improvised tactical Third Army headquarters in Luxembourg day and night on an unscheduled basis. Hasty blackboard sketches supplanted the customary maps in telling the story and in determining enemy capabilities. The chalk diagrams on the board were copied from sketch maps roughly drawn and kept current on sheets of scratch paper. The sketches were sufficient for briefing purposes. Except for inconsequential details, everyone kept himself abreast of the big picture.

Only one of these blackboard briefing sketches remains. It was used at 6:00 A.M. on December 20. Kept at the time for internal evaluation purposes, the sketch is interesting today when compared with actual German plans for the counteroffensive given in the preceding chapter. It is interesting also as a makeshift document, portraying graphically not only all of the capabilities of the enemy that were then apparent, but listing also the "favored" capability. Done on a four-by-seven inch sheet of scrap paper, it was self-explanatory and complete within itself.

The sketch showed seven enemy capabilities. It showed in rough form the configuration of the Bulge as it appeared on that date. Not yet taken were Malmedy, St. Vith, and Bastogne. The enemy capabilities seen were:

(1) To continue the direction of the main effort to the west.

(2) To broaden the shoulders, particularly to the south.

(3) As the main effort lost momentum, to push through with armor to exploit in depth to the west.

(4) Reserve armor to be committed to turn back the shoulders, particularly on the south with a frontal attack in the Echternach area.

(5) If momentum to the west were lost, to launch another main effort to the west or southwest, along or astride the Moselle.

(6) To launch additional small-scale diversionary attacks along Third Army's old front.

(7) To continue small-scale paratroop attacks.

The favored capabilities were (1) and (2), augmented by (3). Capability (5) could become significant at any time, effective that day.

That rough sketch, a copy of which was sent to our intelligence staff at Nancy later that day, was elaborated upon in orthodox fashion and became *Third Army G-2 Estimate No. 11*, dated December 20, 1944. Consisting of seven mimeographed pages, it reflected entirely the views expressed on the blackboard in the Luxembourg briefing early that morning.

The previous day, a preliminary tactical terrain estimate had been made of the area to which the Third Army had just fallen heir. Fortunately, a general terrain study which included that area had been made by Third Army engineers as early as September. It had then been comprehensively done with accompanying plates showing rivers and canals, road networks, railroads, and—as always in Patton's commands—an analysis of suitability of the terrain for what was called "mechanized maneuvers." Its preparation had been based on the Patton inspiration of always being prepared well in advance for almost any eventuality. It had paid off well.

The preliminary tactical terrain estimate pointed up the principal roads, both north-south and east-west, in the area. North-south roads were necessary to the Third Army mission of destroying the enemy on the new north front and being prepared to change directions to the northeast. The east-west routes were those vital to the Germans in their penetration.

The study's last paragraph under a section on military aspects of the terrain was potent. It stated that in approaching the St. Vith area from the south, American use of the Luxembourg-St. Vith road was limited by the enemy's capability to interdict this road north of Ettelbruck. The alternative main road through Arlon, Bastogne, and St. Vith allowed access to both the St. Vith area and the area of the enemy's main penetration. The report concluded that the Bastogne-St. Vith road offered "the best entry into the area."

At about that time, either late on December 19 or early on the twentieth—no diary is available—Patton sent for me. He and General Bradley were standing next to a small wall map in Patton's Luxembourg office. The map was one constantly kept current by his personal staff for his personal information.

Patton, as always, went straight to the point: "Should Bastogne be held?" he asked.

"From an intelligence viewpoint," I responded, "yes."

I then gave a brief resumé of Bastogne's vital importance in the road network system to both the enemy and the Allies, as supported by the recently completed, detailed tactical terrain estimate.

General Patton, looking toward Bradley, nodded affirmation. I departed.

I never knew how much my view contributed to their decision. But Bastogne was held.

As a communications and transportation center, Bastogne was vital to the Germans. The holding of it by American forces spoiled plans for the "Watch on the Rhine." Bypassed, it was sealed off by the Germans on December 21. But it was a paralyzing thorn in their side.

From German accounts, the southern flank defense was being formed according to plan. Bastogne was a part of it. But the Germans had not counted on the swiftness of the American response in defense of Bastogne, nor the valiant spirit of soldiers of the 101st Airborne Division and 10th Armored Division who held out in the encircled city until Patton's III Corps broke through to them on December 26.

Brigadier General Anthony C. McAuliffe's terse "Nuts!" in response to the German demand for the surrender of Bastogne has come to epitomize the heroic efforts of American troops there. By these efforts, the enemy's southern defense line was ruptured and no longer could support the original German plan. Their whole operation was in jeopardy. The Germans made a concerted effort to again seal off Bastogne, but failed. The tide had turned.

We now looked for indications of enemy withdrawal: blown bridges, mine fields, replacing of reconnaissance elements with engineers. The G-2 work map carried the first account of some demolitions at the western tip of the salient on December 28, but who had performed them was not clear.

By the twenty-ninth, the *Third Army G-2 Periodic Report* no longer listed the Germans' continuing advance to the west as a favored capability; instead, it listed only their capabilities against the Third Army Bastogne salient. On the thirty-first, the most feared capability of the enemy, already having reinforced against the Bastogne salient with the equivalent of two Panzer divisions and one infantry division, was that of attacking the shoulders and the base of the salient in an attempt to destroy this increasingly dangerous threat to his lines of communication. This he did with great determination and vigor, but to no avail.

On January 4, two succinct but critically significant reports were made by front-line troops. "Contact with enemy reconnaissance units lost," one said. And shortly thereafter, from the same area, "Enemy engineers identified laying mines."

In mobile offensive operations, reconnaissance units were probers. They felt the way, out front, for the troops following, finding soft spots in enemy resistance along the routes of advance of terrain favorable to forward movement. Combat engineers, on the other hand, could mean either construction or destruction. They paved the way in an advance, or blocked it for defense. They built bridges, or destroyed them. They cleared mine fields or laid them. Mine fields were defensive, used to deny the use of an area to the enemy—not to advancing friendly forces.

So, with reconnaissance reporting the enemy out of contact and mine-laying engineers at work, a major change of German tactics and attitude was immediately apparent. The German advance not only had been slowed, it had been stopped. By their own tactical admission, they were passing from the offense to the defense. This was the beginning of the end of the Battle of the Bulge.

By January 5, we listed the favored enemy capability as that of defending and delaying throughout the Bulge, accomplished by local offensive action spearheaded by armor.* By January 7, the favored capability was withdrawal to a defensive position on the favorable ground extending northeast from Houffalize to St. Vith and from there opposing the Third Army advance to the northeast and/or east. By

---

* Hitler told his high command on January 3 that the offensive no longer was capable of success. On January 7, although some troops had already been forced to withdraw, he permitted publication of the withdrawal order.

the tenth, that capability was still the favored one. It also appeared that the enemy might begin withdrawing the tank elements of his Panzer units and leaving in contact only the infantry elements to defend and delay against American attacks.

*****

From the intelligence viewpoint, the Battle of the Bulge was over. From the overall Third Army viewpoint, the "Bulge" lasted until January 16. On that date the 41st Cavalry of the 11th Armored Division, moving up from the south, made contact with the 41st Infantry of the 2nd Armored Division, driving from the north, in Houffalize.

Although the Bulge ultimately was to prove the Indian Summer of Nazi military might, followed inevitably by its winter of defeat, it was without question one of the most crucial battles of World War II. More than 77,000 American soldiers were left dead, wounded, or captured. The Allied drive on Berlin ground to a halt, granting Russian forces moving on Germany from the east an advantage which in time was to have profound consequences in the division of conquered Europe.

From the outset, it was obvious that the Allied forces had been taken by surprise. Historians have continued to write of the intelligence failure preceding the Bulge. Both General Dwight D. Eisenhower, the top Allied commander, and General Bradley have written that they did not suspect the strength of the German reserve force, nor did they suspect that it might be used *offensively* in the Ardennes. Both had been convinced that Hitler would use whatever reserves he could muster to *defend* in those areas where Allied forces were strongest.

Eisenhower's and Bradley's intelligence staffs—though steeped in the philosophy of judging enemy capabilities and not intentions—apparently were lulled by a similar belief. Unlike that of the British, the established American intelligence procedure was to reserve consideration of enemy intentions for the commander. The intelligence task was to say what the enemy *could* do and let the commander gamble on which of those alternatives the enemy would choose. The enemy capability to launch a strong counteroffensive, regardless of whether it intended to stage one, should have been clearly spelled out to the command.

I talked to Major General Kenneth Strong, Eisenhower's British intelligence officer, in England after the war. During our conversation he asked me, "How did we miss the Bulge?"

When I indicated *we* hadn't, Strong expressed the opinion that his duties had simply been too demanding and that if there ever had been time for him to visit lower headquarters personally maybe such situations wouldn't have developed.

The fact remains, however, that all the intelligence information on which the Third Army G-2 Section based its predictions was available to other commands. Our intelligence reports were widely distributed to higher, lower, and lateral echelons of command. In addition, much of the information which was the basis for our concern came from other units. Abundant information was at hand to support deductions made by the Third Army intelligence staff and clearly outlined in the December 9 briefing at Nancy—a full week before the German offensive began.

Even though the enemy buildup was not on the Third Army front, it was of vital importance to our mission. It was a hard and fast rule in Patton commands that we overlap other areas sufficiently, intelligence-wise, to protect our flanks. While we had no reason to challenge the competence of intelligence received from other quarters, we were simply minding our own business in analyzing and interpreting such reports in the light of our own needs. It was in such analysis and interpretation, apparently, that we differed with other headquarters.

The final outcome of the Battle of the Bulge notwithstanding, the situation was saved by the Allied response *after* the German attack and not by preparations made before. Third Army intelligence reports had accurately adjudged the enemy capabilities and predicted the coming course of events. Had other, higher headquarters taken the precautionary steps that Patton took, the edge of the fanatic Nazi thrust might have been dulled. It could have been von Rundstedt who was taken by surprise as the Allies sprung the trap.

Certainly there was an intelligence failure preceding the Battle of the Bulge. But it was not the total blindness to the enemy buildup which is indicated in prevailing accounts of that historic clash. "Intelligence failure" connotes a breakdown in the intelligence service's collection techniques. The Allied failure leading to the tragedy of the Bulge was in evaluation and application of the intelligence information at hand.

10

THE WINTER OF GERMAN DEFEAT

The small briefing room was filled with visitors. In the front row with Patton were General Eisenhower and other dignitaries. Standing in the rear was Colonel Robert S. Allen, the G-2 chief of operations. I had done the briefing.

The Third Army was preparing for assault. A bold stroke was under discussion: a breakout from the general front along the line north of the Moselle to the Rhine. Third Army forces extended north to south, east of the Kyll River.

General Patton raised a question: "If we seal off the Moselle on the south, how many Germans will be caught between it and the Rhine?"

"Between 20,000 and 25,000 combat effectives," I responded.

No one commented. But everyone shook his head, negatively.

The audience reaction was disturbing. Did they mean my estimates were too high or too low? The head-shaking probably indicated they considered the figures too high.

In the back of the room, Colonel Allen gave the only sign of encouragement. He nodded affirmatively.

It would have been far more comforting if someone present had started a discussion. Then I could have explained that on the order of battle books there were elements and remnants of at least nine German divisions in the area under discussion—none up to strength. Pressed against the Moselle there would be remnants of additional divisions.

The time was early March, 1945. Hitler's last-ditch Ardennes counteroffensive, the Battle of the Bulge, had been turned back. The Allies once again were on the advance, this time to be stopped only by the enemy's unconditional surrender.

The Rhine River was the immediate Allied objective, and after that the German heartland. Time had run out on Hitler's grand plan; the final chapter of the war in Europe began when soldiers of the First United States Army crossed the Remagen Bridge on March 7. The Third Army attack jumped off that same day.

In the next week, 38,572 prisoners of war passed through Third Army cages.

The Third Army chief of staff, General Gay, stopped by to see me.

"You sort of missed that one," he said, smiling. "How many prisoners did you estimate the other day?"

"Twenty- to twenty-five-thousand combat effectives," I replied, also smiling.

"We have already taken more than 35,000 and they're still coming."

"I know," I said, "but I said *combat effectives.*"

We both laughed.

The G-2 estimates for early March had been about 18,000 higher than the number which physically passed through the cages. With this bonus, the books were again in balance. On March 15, with well over 185,000 prisoners taken since the preceding August 1, the actual count varied from our advance intelligence estimates by only 518.

Prisoners of war could prove valuable sources of intelligence information. German soldiers, experience had shown, were remarkably well-informed. Experience had also shown that some were willing to talk. Sometimes *too* willing.

The Third Army intelligence staff would never forget one particular prisoner captured sometime earlier who had told us a convincing story.

His unit had been working on a new and unusual weapon, the PW told interrogators. Then, he said, while he was temporarily away from his post, there had been a terrific explosion. Everything at the site was a shambles and trees in a wide area of the surrounding forest had been laid low. No aircraft had been near and the blast—the most forceful he ever had witnessed—could not possibly have resulted from a bomb.

To add even more intrigue, the soldier was unable to say just what kind of weapon he had been working on. It was so secret that the individuals in his unit never knew the complete story. He knew only enough to be able to carry on his own duties.

The prisoner knew precisely where he was at the time of the blast. He readily pinpointed the exact location on a map.

His story aroused great interest in the intelligence section. The Germans had already launched V-1 and V-2 rockets, and Hitler had promised a "secret weapon" which would one day make its appearance and bring the Allies to their knees. With no other information explaining the explosion, the prisoner's account might very well mark the Allied discovery of a significant new enemy weapon.

The prisoner's story was put through the usual process of challenge. Was the information hearsay? No, it came from an eyewitness. Was the witness reliable? There was no way to know. Was the information confirmed by other sources? No, it was not. Did the information make sense in light of other data at hand? Somewhat.

There was only one loophole in the story. Through calculations of time and space, we concluded that the witness himself should have been caught in the death-dealing blast. But perhaps he had misjudged his own position, an understandable error under the circumstances. In any event, his story was worthy of further investigation. If it turned out to be true, it would be of enormous intelligence significance.

Fortunately, the story could be checked through a relatively simple expedient. If the trees had been laid low over a wide area of the forest as the prisoner said, the effects of the explosion would be readily apparent in aerial photos. Such a mission was requested and flown. The results were awaited with great anticipation.

But the photos showed that all of the trees were still standing; the area was undisturbed. The prisoner's story had been pulled out of the blue.

One of the prisoners taken in the early days of the March offensive, on the other hand, was to prove an extremely valuable source of intelligence information.

"He'll talk," I had been advised, "but only to Patton."

The prisoner was a German major, impressive in appearance and demeanor. The usual tactical questions by battalion, regiment, division, and corps interrogators through which he had been processed had produced nothing. He would talk, he said, "but only to General Patton, in person."

The prisoner arrived at Third Army headquarters with his military escort—but not before plans for his reception had been completed. General Gay had been informed of the situation. So that Patton might not be subjected to the indignities such a meeting might produce, General Gay agreed to act as the commander's stand-in. The prisoner would be received in General Patton's office, but Patton would not be present. It was felt that, although by this time the name of Patton was emblazoned on the minds of all German armies, Patton's physical features probably were not. The German officer would not know the difference.

The stage was set. The prisoner, accompanied by the customary Military Police escort, would be presented to General Gay. I would also be present, along with an interpreter.

The prisoner was brought in. He was obviously an officer of stature, probably Prussian or Junker—erect, monocled, punctilious, heel-clicking, saluting, *"Herr*

General, Jawohl." He appeared to be fiftyish, old for his rank by American standards.

The prisoner's desire to talk, he said, was motivated by patriotism. He had been captured recently, and upon learning that the last barrier to the heart of the German *Reich*—the Rhine—had been breached, he felt that the war should be brought to a speedy end. He was a German, he added, and a good one, willing to do all within his power to save those parts of his country which could still be salvaged. He had information which would contribute vitally to the immediate success of the Allied armies. General Patton, he asserted, was by reputation "a doer." He would make the best use of the information the German was about to reveal.

There was, however, a matter of price. Before he divulged any of this critical material, what price were the Americans willing to pay? Not in terms of dollars, but in terms of protection of his home and family. The way Patton's army moved, he said, his home would be overrun in a matter of days if it hadn't been already. Would the commander guarantee such protection?

"Tell him it would be impossible to guarantee him that his home will not be bombed or that artillery fire will not strike the area," General Gay said to the interpreter. "In war these are impossibilities for reasons he himself must realize. I guarantee him nothing. Our troops are well-disciplined. Their behavior should cause him no concern. If he wants to talk, I'll listen. If not, I consider this interview ended."

The prisoner was hesitant.

"You might also tell him," General Gay continued, "that in all probability we already know anything he intends to tell us anyway."

Obviously somewhat reluctant, the major still wanted to make whatever contribution he could to the saving of his Fatherland. Would he be permitted to spread a map in which "Herr General Patton" would be interested? It was in his briefcase, which his military escort had at hand, he explained.

General Gay cleared a part of his desk.

Spreading the map, the prisoner explained that his duties as a German officer had been concerned with construction. Symbols on his map, he said, marked locations selected by the German high command for construction of proposed military installations as the war progressed. These were to become communications centers housed in bombproof underground shelters. A color code indicated the status of work in progress at the various sites. The map, he added, was current; none of the work had been ordered stopped.

Command requires communications. A marked map showing locations of communications centers would reflect as well the proximity of major headquarters.

And from the location of headquarters sites the future planning of the German high command could be deduced.

If the prisoner's story proved true, the map would be of considerable value not only to the Third Army but also to higher commands. After the interview terminated and all pertinent information was noted, the prisoner was dispatched immediately to the G-2 Section of the Twelfth Army Group.

In view of the possible significance of information gained from the German major, we wanted to check the credibility of his story as quickly as possible. Some of the installations shown on his map were located in the Third Army zone of advance and could be confirmed on the ground in the near future. Until such a time, however, the prisoner's disclosure would be known to only a few persons. Patton, of course, was briefed at once.

On April 6, early in the morning, word was received that advance elements of the 4th Armored Division were approaching Ohrdruf. The closest of the reported secret underground centers would be nearby. Colonel Allen, personally selected for the mission by General Patton, departed for the 4th Armored Division command post. Following a briefing there, he would head a small inspection party which, on the following day, would visit the reported site of the enemy installation to see if things there supported the prisoner's story.

What happened to that ill-fated expedition is a story in itself, told in the succeeding chapter. At the Ohrdruf site, however, they visited the location described by the prisoner. Construction of the underground, bombproof center was complete, although the equipment was not yet operative. Time had obviously been insufficient to allow completion of the installation of the expensive and highly technical equipment. The building had never been occupied. But the site confirmed, at least in part, that the story the German major had told the man he believed to be General Patton was true.

*****

One other thing about the prisoner's map had been of particular interest to the Third Army: it showed no symbol in the area of the Bavarian Alps where, rumor had it, the so-called Alpine Redoubt was being prepared as a fortress where Hitler and his staunchest supporters would make their last stand.

High-level thinking in the spring of 1945 pointed toward the definite possibility that Hitler and his elite would make their last determined stand in the Alps. There was general agreement that occupation of such a final, almost impregnable, center of resistance would be primarily a nuisance—a rallying point for the faithful. But there was also general agreement that if Hitler and his followers did move into the suspected Redoubt they would be in an area in which it would be most difficult to stamp them out.

Our intelligence staff had initiated a plan designed to lead to either final acceptance or final rejection of the growing concern of higher headquarters for the feared Redoubt.

By the very nature of the mountainous terrain and its limited road network, it was an area where provisions for existence would have to be arranged well in advance. The positioning of troops might provide the key to answers on which sound conclusions could be based.

With this objective in mind, we undertook a detailed study of the movements of all SS divisions, going back as far as January. Because of their frenzied loyalty to their *Führer,* the SS—the *Schutzstaffel,* Hitler's elite guard—were most likely to be among those selected for and moved to the final Alps fortress if such were planned.

From January to April 19 when we made our negative conclusions known, we found that not one SS division had been moved to the Alpine area from another front. Certainly, with the parts of the German *Reich* that remained unconquered looking by now like an hourglass with its narrowest middle passage having shrunk to less than one hundred miles east to west near Dresden, some movements would have been made for a last-ditch stand.

One SS mountain division (Andreas Hofer) had been in the Austrian-Italian border area between Innsbruck and Bolzano astride the Brenner Pass for months. The 24th SS Mountain Divison was reported forming northwest of Trieste, and the 14th SS had been reported moving from Czechoslovakia in March to an area near Ljubljana, Yugoslavia. The 16th SS Panzer Division had moved from below Venice to the Czech-Polish border in February and to the south of Graz, Austria, in March and April. No others showed any indication of being available for the occupation of the mountain fastness of the Redoubt. Tactical air reconnaissance found no unusual motor or rail activity supporting reinforcement of the area.

By research and cold analysis, aided by the map data given by the German officer (and now confirmed)—and lacking direct information to the contrary—Third Army intelligence labeled the Redoubt a myth and continued to carry it as such on its books.

Interestingly, if the German high command had any such plans, no record of them ever came to light. Interesting also is the fact that the Germans, inspired by the Allied concern about the Redoubt, played it against the Allies as propaganda with great vigor and telling effect.

They had built up the area in talk, but not in fact.

With time rapidly running out on the Nazi war machine, Patton's Third Army had cleared the Saar and deprived the enemy of his most important industrial areas by late March. Elsewhere along the Third Army front, opposition was limited. Important objectives were taken in rapid succession. Toward the end of March Wiesbaden, Frankfurt, and Weimar were taken, and Erfurt was cleared. On April 14, Third Army troops reached a "restraining line" designated by Bradley west of the Czech border. The general direction of attack was changed from north to southward, Patton's forces regrouping for a move into Czechoslovakia and into Bavaria and Austria.

The Third Army's last campaign of the war started on April 22; two days later the Danube was crossed, Regensburg captured. On May 1 the Inn River was crossed and the Allies entered Austria in strength. Linz and Pilsen were captured.

On May 7, the surrender of all German air, sea, and ground forces was announced, effective at 0001 hours (one minute after midnight) May 9. Patton's forces at the time were closing rapidly toward contact with the Russians on a pre-determined line.

On May 8, General Patton received word that the commanding general of the German Army Group South wanted to discuss the terms of surrender. Patton, instead, delegated that responsibility to me.

"You talk to him," General Patton said. "You know him better than I do; you've been dealing with him for a long time."

*****

Patton's forces held much of the area which became the American occupation zone; he was given command of American occupation troops.

But Patton disagreed strongly with a plan by the Allied high command to create a "sterile" zone around the borders of Germany to isolate the German people. He also favored the quick return to their jobs of key Germans, Nazi or otherwise, to prevent complete economic breakdown and social chaos in the wrecked German nation.

Many Germans who were recognized as Nazis were not Nazis by political choice, Patton maintained in a press conference, but by necessity; one almost had to be a Nazi in wartime Germany to make a living. Unfortunately, he went on to draw an analogy between Nazi Germany and the two-party political system of the United States in which it might be necessary to belong to the party in power and enjoy its patronage to survive bad times.

Amid the clamor raised in the United States by the incident, Patton was reassigned as commander of the Fifteenth Army—a headquarters for which the primary mission was preparation of materials for the historical records of war. It was not an assignment particularly pleasing to a man best suited by temperament to command soldiers in combat.

For weary members of the Third Army staff, however, the end of the war and the later command shift provided a long-desired opportunity for leave time and home visits.

In December, when General Patton died as a result of injuries in a traffic accident in Germany, I was in the States enjoying my first break from military life since the pre-African invasion planning days. I was to have rejoined my old commander and comrade at the end of my leave.

I had been associated with Patton for more than a dozen years. I was present at the awarding of every star in his parade up the ranks to four-star general. At every major command change I had accompanied him. I would not forget him now; I was, and would continue to be, a "Patton man."

HEADQUARTERS SEVENTH ARMY
APO # 758
U.S. Army

22 August 1943

GENERAL ORDER)
                :
NUMBER   18)

Soldiers of the Seventh Army:

Born at sea, baptized in blood, and crowned with victory in the course of 38 days of incessant battle and unceasing labor, you have added a glorious chapter to the history of war.

Pitted against the best the Germans and Italians could offer, you have been unfailingly successful. The rapidity of your dash, which culminated in the capture of Palermo, was equalled by the dogged tenacity with which you stormed Troina and captured Messina.

Every man in the Army deserves equal credit. The enduring valor of the Infantry, and the impetuous ferocity of the tanks were matched by the tireless clamor of our destroying guns.

The Engineers performed prodigies in the construction and maintenance of impossible roads over impassable country. The services of Maintenance and Supply performed a miracle. The Signal Corps laid over 10,000 miles of wire, and the Medical Department evacuated and cared for our sick and wounded.

On all occasions the Navy has given generous and gallant support. Throughout the operation our Air has kept the sky clear and tirelessly supported the operation of the ground troops.

As a result of this combined effort, you have killed or captured 113,350 enemy troops. You have destroyed 265 of his tanks, 2,324 vehicles, and 1,162 large guns, and in addition, have collected a mass of military booty running into hundreds of tons.

But your victory has a significance above and beyond its physical aspect — you have destroyed the prestige of the enemy.

The President of the United States, the Secretary of War, the Chief of Staff, General Eisenhower, General Alexander, General Montgomery have all congratulated you.

Your fame shall never die.

G. S. PATTON, JR.,
Lieut. General, U. S. Army,
Commanding

Patton's congratulatory letter to soldiers of the Seventh Army following victory over German and Italian forces in Sicily. (*U.S. Seventh Army Report of Operations*, "The Seventh Army in Sicily," October 1943)

11

WHAT MAKES A G-2?

What kind of man makes a good intelligence officer? What personal characteristics or professional background should he have? It has been suggested that he must have something distinctive—a little lump somewhere on his head or a certain something that makes him a "natural." Maybe so, but the record fails to prove it.

In civilian life one normally chooses his own field of endeavor; a military officer's choice is usually not so personal. His field is most likely determined for him, and is based on a variety of factors. Education and civilian background weigh heavily in the consideration, but sometimes must be overridden by more pressing needs in a field other than the one indicated.

But given a choice, what personal characteristics or professional backgrounds should be sought in an intelligence officer? Those of lawyers? Analysts? Educators? The prior personal experiences of the personnel of the G-2 sections of the Seventh and Third armies did not point to any particular type or group, encompassing as they did a wide variety and great diversity of backgrounds. They included, along with a very few Regular Army officers, a high school principal, a grade school teacher, two sales representatives, an international banker, a retail salesman of musical instruments, a manufacturer's foreign representative, three journalists, a real estate dealer, a retail shoe salesman, and four lawyers—two of them just out of college.

Yet, even with such greatly varied backgrounds, they had a lot in common. Each possessed imagination, initiative, and mental flexibility. Each was a willing worker, a methodical detail man and organizer. Each was able to work quietly and in harmony with others; none was a worrier, unable to relax.

Every one got along well with and could supervise others, and was able to think on his feet and express himself well.

These qualifications then became the criteria for individual selection of other nominees if and when opportunity presented itself. The reasons to look for these qualities became manifest early.

Imagination, we soon learned, was essential if the intelligence officer were to be able to put himself into the place of the enemy; initiative, if he were to strive constantly to develop new ideas, methods, and techniques and apply them to one of the oldest professions. He had to be a willing worker; intelligence knows no hours. He had to be able to adjust and re-adjust his thinking to meet new and ever-changing situations. He had to have that infinite capacity for painstaking details, for he would find intelligence basically a summary of detail. The intelligence estimate, for example, would be the product of a myriad of details gathered and put into position, one with or against the other, omissions inviting false impressions.

The intelligence officer had to have organizational ability to derive maximum utilization of the personnel and intelligence tools available. He had to plan ahead, setting reasonable and objective completion times for specific projects. To be able to work quietly and harmoniously with others was an absolute necessity because his work usually would be done under the least favorable working conditions possible by men working as a team. Yet, the combat intelligence officer invariably found himself sooner or later in a supervisory position, and he had to be able to handle men.

Under the hectic conditions of the combat situation, it was especially important that members of the G-2 team be able to relax when possible—at least to be able to take their minds off the problems at hand momentarily and look into the future. Time would prove that liaison visits and the exchange of ideas with other headquarters and the gathering of first-hand information under fire at the front provided both useful and refreshing breaks from the confining activities of intelligence work.

Finally, the G-2 team member had to be able to think on his feet. At any time he might be called upon to express his views. Whether before his peers or in the presence of high rank, he must do so with precise accuracy and with the courage of his convictions.

And, in addition to all these qualifications—a big order in themselves—it was found that the intelligence officer needed an abundance of honest-to-goodness, matter-of-fact, feet-on-the-ground common sense!

Tactical training was desirable for all in the intelligence section. An intelligence officer with training in armor, for example, could best analyze the items of enemy armor significance. Training with troops had an added advantage. From their personal experience, officers with such training would know that a seemingly simple staff directive is often difficult to carry out. Only then could they visualize the impact of a few written or spoken words on the ultimate recipients—the men in combat.

The concept of a G-2 *team* was of critical importance. No one individual could handle all intelligence affairs and provide all the answers to all the questions about all the things which were a direct G-2 responsibility. I soon learned that the more matters I tried to handle personally, the more I became engulfed in detail, usually losing in the process the larger picture which had to be my primary concern. An intelligence staff—a G-2 Section—had to be provided. For Patton's Third Army, the section consisted of sixteen officers and warrant officers and twenty-five enlisted men.

The G-2 team was built upon specialization. Whether in planning or in actual operations, it always embraced six major components, the designations of which were most readily identified by their primary activities: administration, combat intelligence, security, photo and map, auxiliary agencies, and an executive group.

The administration branch, in general, was charged with all business administration—the paper work, supplies, transportation, and reproduction and dissemination of intelligence publications. More specifically, it operated the G-2 message center, maintained the section's files, prepared requisitions for both personnel and supplies, ran the mimeograph machines, kept tabs on the transportation and its maintenance, arranged for the physical dissemination of documents (whether by foot, jeep, or air), and consolidated the monthly G-2 branch reports into the G-2 historical "after-action" reports required by regulations.

The combat intelligence branch was charged primarily with the collection of information and its processing and publication. To accomplish this mission it kept G-2 situation and work maps; kept the G-2 journal and its accompanying work sheets; prepared intelligence summaries, bulletins, and other publications of intelligence interest; prepared the G-2 estimates and periodic reports; made target area analyses; conducted research and maintained a reference file for that purpose; arranged for liaison visits to other headquarters; conducted the G-2 briefings, and was charged with the organization and supervision of the war room with its maps and charts. Its order of battle personnel were the experts on enemy organization, strength, location, disposition, equipment, and tactics.

The security branch was charged with arrangements for keeping all information and intelligence from reaching the enemy by any source. Specifically, its interests were mostly "counter": counterespionage, countersabotage, countersubversion. It prepared counterintelligence directives, published counterintelligence information, maintained counterintelligence files, established counterintelligence control lines, and maintained files on personalities in enemy-controlled areas. It arranged for passwords and replies, published censorship guidances, supervised intelligence funds, and made periodic checks of military and document security.

The photo and map branch was charged with all intelligence matters relating to production of intelligence from the results of visual and air photo reconnaissances— its requirements, and interpretation and publication of its results. It prepared the map requirements of the command and set map policies, assisted in preparation of tactical terrain analyses and in the dissemination of weather information.

The auxiliary agencies branch was in charge of the supervision, briefing, coordination, and administration of all attached or assigned auxiliary agencies—such specialists as interrogators of prisoners of war, interpreters, instructors in evasion and escape techniques, experts in psychological warfare, enemy documents personnel, and groups representing clandestine activities such as the OSS and its counterparts in other Allied forces. To insure coverage it allocated some of these intelligence specialists to lower echelons of command and made detailed arrangements for the exploitation of their specialties at the headquarters to which they were attached. As appropriate, these specialists collected and prepared reports from captured enemy personnel or through the seizure, examination, and analysis of enemy documents.

My assistant G-2 and I formed the sixth component of the G-2 team, the executive group. Our chief responsibilities were along the lines of policy-making, coordination, and supervision. The effectiveness of the intelligence team was my responsibility. Within the headquarters I attended all staff meetings and all briefings in which the G-2 Section participated. I personally briefed the commanding general or chief of staff on a day-to-day basis and maintained contact with chiefs of other sections in the headquarters. I made personal liaison visits to other headquarters as often as possible.

*****

One of the key members of Patton's Third Army intelligence team, as noted earlier, was Colonel Robert S. Allen, better known for his civilian endeavors as the journalist who at one time co-authored with Drew Pearson the newspaper political column, "Washington Merry-go-Round." As an officer in the Wisconsin National Guard, Allen had been graduated from the old Cavalry School at Fort Riley, Kansas. When called to active duty as a major in early 1942, he requested duty with the troops (rather than in a public relations post which could logically be expected for a journalist of his stature). He was granted that request and assigned to Lieutenant General Walter Krueger's Third Army headquarters at Fort Sam Houston, Texas. Sent then to the Command and General Staff School at Fort Leavenworth, Kansas, he was reassigned upon graduation to the Third Army G-2 Section.

In the States, Allen conducted a series of combat intelligence schools in the Third Army maneuver areas and devised intelligence proficiency tests for Army units alerted for overseas combat. When the Third Army moved to England in 1944 to become General Patton's command in Europe, Allen was the executive officer of the G-2 Section.

It was Colonel Allen who, in the spring of 1945, was personally selected by Patton to head an intelligence inspection team to test the credibility of the captured German officer's report on plans of the German high command for establishment of a series of communications centers, as mentioned in the preceding chapter. Specifically, Allen was charged with the responsibility for pinpointing locations of the alleged installations and personally checking out the sites.

On April 6, 1945, reports were received that advance elements of the Third Army were approaching the first of those sites, Ohrdruf. Colonel Allen, accompanied by two other officers of the Third Army staff, immediately departed for the 4th Armored Division command post at Gotha. What they found at Ohrdruf bore out the German officer's testimony. The prisoner had also reported another installation in the Wechmar area some six miles north of Ohrdruf, where the sketchy information we had at hand showed an extremely fluid battle situation. An inspection of the enemy communications installation there, if it were found, could add important information to the intelligence picture: Was the installation finished? Could it have been in operation?

Colonel Allen's party of seven—five from Third Army Headquarters and two from the 4th Armored Division—left Ohrdruf that morning in a three-jeep convoy. All were armed with individual weapons. Two of the jeeps were armed with light machine guns, none with radio. At Wechmar they were advised that friendly armored columns had passed through without encountering the enemy. They proceeded to the outskirts of town, where American tanks were parked on either side of the road. Handwave greetings were exchanged. The area seemed to be as secure as a fluid offensive situation could make it.

The planned route led through the small village of Apfelstadt, which was reached without incident. No one was in the streets, although it was a bright and sunny Saturday afternoon. Doors were closed, windows shuttered. The deathly quiet was noted with apprehension. It followed the pattern of other villages through which enemy troops had recently passed—or were expected to pass soon—and offered countless opportunities for sniper fire. Because the centuries-old, narrow, and winding streets had frequent "blind" right-angle turns, the jeeps and their occupants were seldom within sight of one another. They continued through the village at a cautious fifteen miles per hour at approximately seventy-five-yard intervals.

As the lead vehicle made one such sharp turn, its occupants spotted a bicyclist in the uniform of the *Volks Sturm,* civilian clothing with a distinctive arm band. As the cyclist made a rapid exit from the town, the jeep driver accelerated to overtake him. The following jeeps likewise increased their speed. The cyclist left the road and pedaled rapidly toward a small shed a few hundred yards away, across an open field, with the American jeep in pursuit. Only as the jeep neared the shed did the occupants notice the cluster of some fifteen German soldiers there. The other two jeeps had by this time closed to within a short distance of the lead vehicle, and all three came quickly to a halt. The Germans obviously had been taken by complete surprise; the officer in the lead jeep opened on them with machine gun fire. The enemy soldiers, taking cover in a nearby ditch, returned the fire. The American gunner fell heavily to the ground, mortally wounded. The other Americans were now out of their jeeps and firing from positions prone on the ground. The Germans attempted no advance.

When a second group of enemy soldiers opened fire from a hedge to their rear, members of the small American force found themselves in an extremely difficult position. Colonel Allen, firing his submachine gun, suffered a blast of a half dozen rounds in his right arm, shattering the elbow. One of the drivers crawled toward the third jeep, mounted it, and after firing a short machine gun blast fell backward with a grave wound in the stomach. The efforts of the driver of the second vehicle were more successful. He managed to turn his jeep around and race it clear of the area, mounted on the run by one of the remaining officers. These two escaped, immediately recounting their experiences at the command post at Gotha. By evening, headquarters of the Third Army had been informed.

Colonel Allen was found by his captors in a partially water-filled ditch. A tourniquet was applied by a German in civilian clothes wearing a Red Cross armband. The wounds were wrapped with paper dressings. A German non-commissioned officer then had the prisoner placed in one of the captured American jeeps, but when Allen's rank as a colonel was recognized he was transferred to a German vehicle and taken directly to the German barracks in Erfurt. There the incident was reported to an officer presumed to be a general, who gave orders that Allen be hospitalized locally and that his capture be reported immediately to the corps headquarters at Weimar. Transported to another building in the compound, he was then walked in his bloodsoaked boots to an improvised operating room in the cellar.

In Vienna in 1949 his Austrian surgeon filled in the story. He remembered Colonel Allen well. And he remembered the circumstances under which he had operated upon the American officer. Times were bad for the German Army, he said. The war should have been over months before. While Hitler's was a political cause of which he had no part, he said he had had no choice but to serve in the German Army—and he had served honestly and faithfully. As a doctor, however, he had devoted his life to saving life; politics, he had determined, could, should, and would be separate from his medical profession.

The military situation was fluid, the Austrian surgeon recalled. Wounded were streaming in. When this critically hurt American officer appeared, the question of emergency priorities had to be determined. The prisoner's right arm required immediate emergency surgery: amputation above the elbow. The doctor's decision to give first priority to this American colonel whose lifeblood was fast ebbing away was later criticized by his German superiors as "preferential" treatment.

By conventional standards the operating room was totally inadequate. With the facility functioning on an all-out emergency basis, there had been little time for customary cleanups. Bloody bandages lay where they had been snipped off; what sterilizing was possible was reserved for the wounds proper. For lack of medicants, the usual anesthetic procedures had long since been abandoned. A patient could still be given enough anesthesia to carry him through the major portion of his surgery, but no more. The refinement of the patient's still being unconscious while surgical dressings were applied was no longer possible. After that, some cognac, a few pain tablets, and some sleeping pills were all that would be available to numb the pain.

Early on the morning of April 8, the day after Colonel Allen's surgery, he was visited by the doctor. Barring infection, he was told, there should be no complications. The dressings would be changed in two or three days. He learned that during the night surgery had been performed on an American sergeant—one shot through the stomach. Also, he was told that a German intelligence officer from higher headquarters had arrived during the night and demanded to talk to Colonel Allen. This permission, after some discussion, the surgeon had denied.

"I demand the right," the officer had persisted.

"I refuse," had been the doctor's reply. And there it had stood. "Come back in a few days."

Before the "few days" passed, the Austrian surgeon was to hear rumblings of his disloyalty to the Nazi cause. But those rumblings must have been accompanied by equally sinister ones—the Third Army on the march. Distantly, shellfire was heard; more closely, aerial bombardment.

A Berliner arrived. "I have come to accompany Colonel Allen to higher head-quarters," he advised the surgeon. Informed that the patient could not be moved, the Berliner responded curtly, "We cannot be permitted to stand on medical ceremony. You are under arrest."

"Why?"

"You will be informed. Tomorrow, without fail, Colonel Allen will be moved to Berlin—dead or alive."

Later in the day, a higher ranking German medical officer appeared and asked Colonel Allen why he had been subjected to this unusual preferential treatment. Didn't he know the wonders of German medicine and medical ethics? And, he wanted to know, why were Britain and the United States making common cause with the Soviets? All of this he asked in German, which Allen spoke well.

After his departure, Colonel Allen's nurse, an Evangelical sister, informed him that strict orders had been given that henceforth he was to have no visitors—he had had none—and that he was under constant surveillance. After dark an air alarm sounded and the patient, accompanied by his nurse and several soldiers, was removed to a shelter in the cellar. The cellar was packed with patients, nurses and other members of the hospital staff, and civilians. Among them Allen saw for the first time, though only at a distance, the wounded American jeep driver.

American fighter-bombers had continually attacked a German gun position on a wooded hillside near the hospital all afternoon. Now they had turned to the railroad marshalling yards in Erfurt, while American artillery took under fire a military compound in the vicinity of the hospital. The hospital was not hit, but concussions from the exploding shells could be strongly felt.

About noon the next day, April 10, word spread rapidly that the Americans were on the outskirts of town, encircling it. Communications had been cut, it was reported, and the Germans in Erfurt were now out of contact with those to the east.

Colonel Allen was told that three additional American wounded had been brought in during the night and that they were getting such care as could be provided. One case was serious and an emergency operation had been performed.

That afternoon the senior German medical officer appeared again, his attitude greatly changed. This time he was solicitous. How was *Herr Oberst* getting along? Did he need or want anything?

Now it was Colonel Allen's turn. He had noted arms and ammunition in the hospital building and that weapons were being worn and carried—a direct violation of the rules of the Geneva Convention.

"As the senior American officer in the hospital," he stated, "I assume command. Inform all that they are, as of now, American prisoners of war. Machine weapons, grenades, and other ammunitions are to be collected and locked in the basement. Sidearms, daggers, and the like are to be collected, boxed, and placed under lock and key."

And incidentally, he continued, the Nazi salute was not considered proper. While he would not presume to lay down regulations as to how they saluted among themselves, when they saluted Americans it would be in an acceptable military manner. Other than that, all would continue their normal duties.

"*Jawohl,* " the German medical officer replied.

As soon as the first American troops entered the building, Colonel Allen went on, they would be informed of his presence and be reported to him in person. "And one more thing—that surgeon I release from arrest."

At about 4:00 A.M. on April 11, Colonel Allen was informed that an American patrol had entered the hospital. One of its soldiers made a bedside report that Erfurt was occupied. A short time later a lieutenant from the 1st Battalion, 318th Infantry, of the 80th Infantry Division appeared. Colonel Allen directed that Third Army headquarters be informed immediately of his whereabouts and safety, and that safe passage be arranged immediately for his Austrian surgeon to visit his aged and dependent parents elsewhere in overrun Germany.

Within an hour, evacuation of all the American wounded through 80th Division medical channels was underway. Colonel Allen was flown back by Army liaison plane to a station hospital in the vicinity of the Third Army command post at Hersfeld.

At the first opportunity, General Patton paid him a visit. Allen, he found, had two anxious questions. Could he be permitted to return to his old job as an assistant G-2? Could he be permitted to stay with the Third Army until the war's end? Ground rules, General Patton explained, called for the immediate dispatch of all repatriated American prisoners of war to the continental United States. An exception would require the personal approval of General Eisenhower. But maybe it could be arranged.

It was. On April 23, after a total absence of only seventeen days, Colonel Robert S. Allen—now left-handed—was back at his desk doing full military duty, asking no favors and receiving none.

"...The courage and sense of obligation and devotion to duty which prompted you after being badly wounded to avoid evacuation to the rear and to return to your duties is in the best tenets of the military service...." So read General Patton's commendation.

12

INTELLIGENCE IN COMBAT

Combat intelligence in World War II grew with necessity. Army intelligence publications totaled only about two dozen when troops of the United States first entered the war in 1942, despite earnest efforts in this direction when it became obvious that American entry into the war was inevitable. As late as 1939 there had been only four such publications. By war's end, however, combat intelligence was a vastly improved military science. Necessity had become the mother of invention. When a new need became obvious, some means was devised to meet that need. If it worked well, it was likely to be adopted as standard practice. In the commands of General Patton, the intelligence seed planted in North Africa took root in Tunisia, matured in Sicily, blossomed in France, and bore fruit across the Continent.

Even as new intelligence techniques and practices were found and improved upon, the basic processes remained the same: direction, collection, collation, evaluation, interpretation, and dissemination. But the efficiency with which these processes were accomplished grew with the experience of those of us who were charged with that responsibility.

Intelligence errors in combat, if serious, were measured in terms of lives lost. If they led to wrong tactical decisions, an intelligence officer was readily available for reassignment. Short of this kind of mistake, however, he was in a good position to "wait and see," to compare estimates with actual occurrences to see if and where they differed. If he had missed any bets he could check again to determine what available intelligence resources he had failed to use, sources which, with a little more ingenuity and foresight, he might have used to gain the missing information.

Basically, the intelligence officer's job was to supply his commander's EEIs. This was the direction his efforts had to take, to supply his commander with the information necessary to make the command decisions critical to fulfillment of the mission. From there on, however, the intelligence business was his alone. He and his staff would be charged with finding the right sources of information, sorting bits and pieces together until an overall picture developed, then evaluating and interpreting the information at hand in light of other known facts and seeing that the resulting intelligence reached the right people.

It was his responsibility to determine who could best get what. To this end he had to check not only his own resources, but also those of higher, lower, and adjacent echelons of command and even of other services. What were the offshore beach conditions in a planned invasion area? The answer would be determined by the Navy, stealthily launching rubber boats from submarines. Where were the inland exits from beach areas? Get aerial photos. Were there new enemy troops in contact? Ask the front line troops, the PW interrogators. Was there a buildup in enemy artillery? Ask the artillery officer, or the liaison-type aircraft observers, or counterbattery intelligence officers, or prisoners. Were Panzers on the move? Ask the tactical air reconnaissance pilots. Check with radio intercept units. Was that latest shell fired into the command post a new and hitherto unused and unknown weapon? Ask the artillery intelligence team specialists who would analyze the shell fragments.

The intelligence officer had to prepare careful plans for directing the efforts of his collecting agencies. Overlapping had to be avoided, except that which was necessary for confirmation. No collection agency should be overloaded with too many high-priority items. Sometimes the directions might not call for specific information, but for ideas instead. Such a contribution might point the way to new and previously unrecognized sources.

Sources of information, we soon learned, were as many and as varied as the items on which information was sought. Sources were limited only by the individual intelligence officer's ingenuity in exploiting them. Insignia on enemy uniforms provided unit identifications—and so did the letter from home abandoned in slit trench or bunker. The turret on a tank told the model, the thickness of its armor plate, its vulnerability. Marked maps taken from the enemy dead gave disposition of troops, communications, further plans of an operation. An individual soldier's ration might provide information on the status of the enemy's supply situation; so might an overrun supply dump. Shell fragments could provide virtually the same information as a captured artillery piece. Interrogation of prisoners of war could reveal crucially important information; so could remarks overheard among the civilian population. Air reconnaissance photographs told graphically what needed to be known about a particular site. Hastily drawn field sketches and picture post cards* could do likewise. The more obvious sources of information were explored through routine collection agencies provided for that purpose. Unusual sources, on the other hand, were explored by whatever means possible whenever and wherever recognized. No stone under which a bit of information might be located was left unturned. Opportunity might not knock again; in fact, it usually didn't.

The collection of intelligence information began with the front line soldier. The division, no matter whether infantry, armor, or airborne, was the keystone to combat intelligence in World War II. It was a collector of information, indispensable and irreplaceable. The division took prisoners of war. It picked up enemy deserters. It overran enemy wounded and dead. It sent out patrols. It seized enemy command posts, manned observation posts, and established listening posts. It captured enemy materiel. It had reconnaissance platoons and companies and battalions. It had within its own organization the available assistance and support of the intelligence sections of its varied units, plus the professional know-how of ordnance, signal, chemical, and engineer experts. It was, in short, the division which was the best equipped to provide intelligence information gained through physical contact with the enemy.

What the division lacked in collecting enemy information was usually provided by attached intelligence specialists who served as extremely efficient helping hands. Each division had at least fifty auxiliary intelligence specialist personnel attached in the form of teams. Normally included were tactical interrogators of prisoners of war, enemy order of battle specialists, military intelligence interpreters, translators, air photo interpreters, and CIC personnel.

The corps would have at least twice as many specialist teams as its divisions, including the same types plus others, better organized and equipped to serve a larger command: a mobile weather detachment which could forecast weather for the entire corps area, for example, and specialized engineers with map reproduction facilities.

By the time all these teams were totaled up at the field army headquarters, the number of attached specialists rarely fell below 2,000—and on many occasions it was double that number. Those units attached directly to the army headquarters

* In preparing for the invasion of French Morocco in 1942, Taskforce Blackstone planners, still in the States, located a critically needed assault beach near Safi through a picture post card. The Navy had made a special project of collecting any and all types of beach and waterfront pictures available, from any source, and cataloging and filing them in Washington.

would again include the same types as were attached to division and corps headquarters, plus those whose duties, broader in scope, would more adequately augment intelligence resources at that level. Here would be found teams designed to process enemy documents in volume; evasion and escape experts who would instruct the troops in how to evade capture or how to escape if they were captured; special air interrogators for downed enemy air force personnel; mobile interrogation units which served strategic purposes rather than front line tactical needs, and OSS detachments.

All of these auxiliary agencies normally were responsible directly to the chief intelligence officer. They were as varied in size as in purpose, on occasion ranging from three-man teams to detachments equivalent in size to a battalion of artillery or a cavalry group with two or more mechanized squadrons.

Other intelligence attachments operated under their own headquarters staff sections. Signal intelligence, for example, operated through the office of the army signal officer. Relationships in liberated or occupied areas were under the civil affairs or military government staff chief. Technical intelligence teams operated under the respective chiefs of the sections whose names identified their specialties: artillery, surgeon (for medical), ordnance, engineer, chemical, transportation corps, quartermaster, and signal. All had a direct interest in enemy techniques and equipment in their special technical fields. Psychological warfare detachments and the field press censors were the responsibility of the political and psychological warfare chief (at one time "G-6," a short-lived designation), as was the public relations section, later more appropriately called public information. All required close coordination with G-2 activities.

The Air Warning Services and several reporting systems employed to keep contact with friendly troops were of vital interest to intelligence but operated under the G-3 Section.

Army Group headquarters attached advanced documents sections and censorship personnel, the former for rapid scrutiny and strategic evaluation of bulky captured documents, and the latter broken down into activities concerning the Allied press, base censorship for military and PW mail, and censorship of the civilian postal, telephone, and telegraph system if operations were in an enemy country.

Initially, the attached auxiliary agency teams were not popular with tactical commanders. The tactical commander was interested primarily in results which had a direct bearing on immediate tactical problems. As collectors of information, however, every one of his attachments sooner or later would pay its way. Each would, at one time or another, furnish basic intelligence information on which a tactical decision would be based. And once they proved themselves they not only were welcome, they were in demand.

Army headquarters was the lowest headquarters in the field in charge of the coordination with supporting Tactical Air Command of all matters pertaining to ground force requests for air tactical and photo reconnaissance. Air photo reconnaissance was relatively new in the early days of the war, at least in terms of advanced techniques. Direct application to military needs had been slow. Photo interpreters were practically nonexistent.* But it was soon learned that a myriad of intelligence information could be gained from a single air photograph—not only the presence of enemy troops and installations, but also such less obvious things as type of vegetation, length of a bridge, presence of mine fields, and the type and caliber of weapons. Even the height of a building could be determined by computing the length of its shadow.

Although the specialized nature of visual and photo reconnaissance from the air gained deserved recognition early in the war, it was not until 1944 that the staff section charged with exploiting these valuable sources of enemy information gained formal recognition. It was then that a "G-2 Air" section became an authorized intelligence branch at each army and corps headquarters in the commands of the First Army Group in England. Until then, each G-2 Section simply had to devise its own makeshift procedures for exploiting air reconnaissance techniques, using whatever personnel were available.

The new arrangement was obviously a great improvement. It created a recognized G-2 branch which henceforth was responsible for the production and dissemination of all intelligence resulting from air reconnaissance. It would coordinate all air reconnaissance requests, interpret all air photos, and publish the results. It would brief and interrogate the pilots through authorized—and well-trained—ground liaison officers (GLOs), who could now be accommodated more conveniently at the air field.

The head of G-2 Air was not an officer of the Air Corps. He had to be an experienced Army officer with special technical qualifications. He had to be entirely familiar with Army organization, tactics, and techniques. He had to know what would be of direct concern to the ground forces. He had to be able to interpret air photos, not only to supervise his photo interpreters intelligently but also to be able to make spot interpretations himself on occasion when hasty information was

---

* In the planning days for the Moroccan invasion, only one officer of desired military stature and staff experience who could interpret air photos efficiently could be found in the entire 2nd Armored Division. He was Colonel Harold M. Forde, a 1926 graduate of the United States Military Academy at West Point who had also served at the Academy as an instructor in that subject.

needed by the commander—when on-the-spot tactical decisions had to be made in the field from a few photos at hand. He had to be a qualified intelligence officer. At the same time, his knowledge of applicable Air Corps capabilities and limitations had to be sufficient to permit him to converse intelligently with air experts.

The pilot of the reconnaissance airplane was a busy man. In flight, he had to recognize and differentiate between friendly and enemy infantry, armor, and artillery and to pinpoint them on the ground. In amphibious operations, he had to differentiate between friendly and enemy naval craft. He had to make quick estimates of the size of enemy units in bivouac, on the march, or in tactical formation. Simultaneously, he had to determine the enemy's anti-aircraft potential, reporting flak both as to intensity and caliber. Meanwhile, he had to keep an eye open for enemy aircraft.

The ground liaison officers assisted in the pilots' briefings at the airfield before takeoff and with their interrogations upon return. From the ground viewpoint they interpreted the observations made in flight. At least three officers usually performed GLO duty, one each of infantry, armor, and artillery. They were always furnished the EEIs, which they in turn passed on to the pilots. They acted as counselors as to what to look for, what it should look like, and, in general, where to look.

Whenever practical, front line units would listen in on the reconnaissance aircrafts' radio transmissions and hear directly what the pilots were reporting. Transmissions were limited mostly to "flash" reports, through which anything of immediate value to the front lines would be given them first-hand without passing through the regular, more time-consuming channels.

The growth of air photography in the collection of intelligence information was almost phenomenal. In Tunisia, two photographic air missions were flown in support of Patton's II Corps in a thirty-day period in January and February, 1943. This number increased to six in the next month, and jumped to thirty in the last three weeks of the campaign. A total of 140 missions were flown in support of the Seventh Army during the thirty-eight days of Sicilian operations. By the end of August, 1944, the first month in which it was operational on the Continent, the Third Army had received 3,365,287 air photo prints. In September, 223 photo missions were flown, producing more than a half-million prints. And in December, during the Battle of the Bulge, air photos produced from negatives taken early in September (before the area was first overrun by Allied troops) were dropped into Bastogne and immediately put to use. The negatives had prudently been stored in England. In the single month of March, 1945, a total of 1,342,517 air photo prints were handled through the Third Army Photo Center.

A few months before the end of the war in Europe, the War Department issued orders creating a special staff section at army level—the Army Air Section. It was designed to bring all of the field army's air interests into one section by combining G-2 Air and G-3 Air. In the Third Army, however, it was felt that the move offered little or no improvement over what had developed naturally as the most efficient system. The two sub-sections were combined on paper according to the newly-authorized tables of organization, but remained physically with the G-2 and G-3 sections where they had been all along.

The OSS also played an important role in the collection of intelligence information. When beach studies were vitally needed during intelligence planning for the invasion of southern France, they were obtained by the OSS. Were the beach defenses strong? A request was placed with the OSS. How long would it take? Ten days to two weeks. Within that period, a complete outline of the defenses, drawn to scale on a map with draftsman precision and ready for reproduction was given to me personally. Instead of the scrawled notes I'd expected, the whole thing arrived neatly folded and in a suitcase! Details of how the task was accomplished were never known.*

The effects of the terrain under enemy control on a commander's mission was a G-2 concern, as was the weather. Depending upon the size of the command, specific interests might include terrain features ranging from mountains and forests down to individual trees and hummocks. Likewise, concern with the weather might range from the broad effects of climate on the availability of supplies to whether there would be a moon on a given night. Both terrain and weather were always matters of comprehensive intelligence study. Military maps were the foundation of terrain estimates. Map data was supplemented by whatever additional information became available concerning soil conditions, vegetation, and the like. Locations of cities and villages could be of critical importance, as could the locations of rivers and streams, highways and railroads, and canals—in tactical terms, the natural lines of movement. The actual contour of the land could be estimated fairly accurately from a good map, even if it didn't carry such information; winding rivers, streams, highways, or railroads were a good indication of hilly countryside where steep banks and gorges could be expected.

Particularly in planning, relief models showing the ground as it would be seen in actual contour were of great assistance. In the field, especially in the earlier days

---

* It was precisely at this time that I finally got around to reading a book, Emil Ludwig's *The Mediterranean,* received as a Christmas gift. By an astonishing coincidence, one of the first references I discovered was to a lighthouse on one of the Hyere Islands, a site that was at that very moment of great intelligence interest.

of the war, terrain models were usually made with plaster of Paris and were heavy and bulky. Varying colors were used when color was available. In emergencies, iodine and Mercurochrome obtained through medical channels were used as paint substitutes. Later in the war, terrain models made of rubber were furnished. These were light and easy to carry, and could be rolled up when not in use.

Regardless of whatever success we might have achieved in the collection of information, such information was of little use until it reached the right hands. Corps and higher headquarters intelligence officers were each charged with the responsibility for keeping their next higher headquarters informed of information received from the lower echelons by means of the "ISUM," as described earlier. All headquarters were responsible for passing information up and to other headquarters which might have an interest in it, through "spot" reports. There was always a time lag between the time of an event and the time it was reported, of course, the amount of time dependent upon the distances involved and type of transmission used. But a constant flow of information was desired and information gained was information lost unless it was reported promptly.

By the same token, intelligence material was of little use until put in its proper perspective in an overall view with other information at hand. Information became intelligence only after evaluation and interpretation. Information was evidence; evidence must be weighed and judged by the jury. This involved an appraisal of the estimated value and quality of reports received and the reliability of respective sources—a process of challenge. How was the information obtained? Was it confirmed by other sources? Did it make sense when placed alongside data already at hand? At some point in this challenging process, the information would have to be accepted, rejected, or placed in a questionable status to await further evidence.

It was essential that intelligence information, once accepted, be catalogued in some form where it was readily available and graphically apparent. In each intelligence section, regardless of echelon, a G-2 situation map (work map) was kept current. Data on the enemy was posted as it was received, twenty-four hours a day. It provided the most graphic picture possible with the information we had of the enemy at any given time. The size of the unit keeping the map determined what information was posted. In lower headquarters the maps were of sufficiently large scale to permit great detail, while on the army headquarters map enemy strength most likely would be reflected in no greater detail than division.

To avoid constant replacing of the work maps—even if available, which they usually were not—the basic map was covered with a transparency (acetate if available, otherwise translucent tracing paper). As posted items lost their significance in light of more current reports, changes and deletions were necessary. Before changes were made, a copy of the posted map was made on an overlay. The old data then expunged, the copied overlay augmented the data in the *G-2 Periodic Report,* which had faithfully reduced the same information to the written record.

Early in 1944, photographers in the Third Army signal section developed a system for photographing the G-2 situation map, which, at that headquarters, was never smaller than six feet square. This not only overcame the tedious task of copying, but also eliminated the problem of filing the bulky paper overlays. The whole thing was now reduced to an eight by ten inch photo. Of even greater importance, additional copies could readily be made and disseminated. It was photographed daily, immediately after midnight to coincide with the closing time of the *G-2 Periodic Report,* and copies were distributed by daylight.

Ultimately, a photocopy of the G-2 situation map became the standard cover for the Third Army *G-2 Periodic Report.*

Again, a unit commander could see the enemy situation at a glance and his G-2 was spared the hurried but detailed plotting on his own maps of significant items covered in greater detail in the report proper.

Of all the published routine intelligence reports prepared during operations, the *G-2 Periodic Report* was the most formal. It was published and issued daily covering a twenty-four-hour period, immediately following a closing hour specified by its next higher headquarters. Finding its way into the archives, it would record for posterity the enemy activities during the period. Characteristically, it was brief, clear, to the point, pertinent to the situation—an evaluated and interpreted summary of the enemy situation.

Issued in general by divisions, corps, and armies, the *G-2 Periodic Report* was widely distributed—to higher, lower, and lateral headquarters, to special troops serving under or attached to its own headquarters, and to staff sections with the headquarters. Distribution of the division-level report usually required twenty-five to thirty-five mimeographed copies, the army-level report requiring 150. Not all the information in the report would be new to all recipients, some of it having been disseminated earlier as "spot" reports.

Like other intelligence tools, the *G-2 Periodic Report* grew in stature as the war progressed. While earlier reports might have run two or three pages, the Third Army report covering the period of midnight, December 30, 1944, through the next twenty-four hours consisted of twenty-four pages, including the annexes, which embraced seven pages of tactical interrogation of prisoners of war, two pages of data on defenses as reported through civilian and OSS sources, two pages of order of battle identifications in the Third Army zone of advance, and four pages of significant order of battle facts. An additional "Stop Press" note added after the closing hour noted a ground source report that the 2nd SS Panzer Division had just moved from the First Army zone to a location in front of the Third Army.

Accompanying the report were maps showing the enemy order of battle data for the western front (by then a weekly feature) and a set of over-printed maps plotting detailed results of aerial reconnaissance and photo interpretations covering the ten-day period of December 22-31.

The distribution of maps was another important G-2 Section function. We established the mapping policies and determined how many copies of each were necessary and to whom they should go. The engineers did the reproduction and distribution and the volume was staggering. Early in the war, the Western Task Force had sixty tons of maps prepared for the invasion of French Morocco. These million sheets of paper would eventually be broken down by count to such relatively low numbers as two here and six there, to be packaged and delivered to assigned units. Although refinements and innovations eliminated production of many special-interest maps (combining many types of special information on one map), Third Army action in the Battle of the Bulge still required issue of fifty-seven tons of maps during the ten-day period beginning December 18. Thirty tons of maps were issued by Third Army engineers in the first eight days of May, 1945, and the war ended with more than 130 tons of map paper still on hand in Third Army warehouses.

The *G-2 Estimate of the Situation* was the formal written vehicle used to determine the enemy capabilities. It consisted of two parts—a summary of the enemy situation immediately preceding its publication, and a set of conclusions reached through an analysis of that summary. The summary section was a recitation of enemy activity, location, and activities in forward and rear areas, the terrain as it affected him, and the probable effect of weather on him. Enemy capabilities were listed in the estimate in the order in which they became apparent and were numbered in that order, not in any order of preference. Time permitting, each senior member of the G-2 staff contributed his thoughts and ideas. And, time permitting, particularly in the planning stages of an operation, war gaming was highly desirable to assist in reaching conclusions. In war games both friendly and enemy forces were portrayed and represented by members of the staff. Each side reacted as it most logically would with the troops and means at hand if actually engaged on the ground in combat against the other.

In the formal estimate, each enemy capability was, in its turn, discussed pro and con in writing. If other capabilities suggested themselves in this discussion, they were added. One, or several in combination, emerged as the most logical to be adopted by the enemy. It was given preference over the others by dint of reasoning and became the "favored" capability. The discussion concluded with a justification for its adoption, giving the reader the background of the thinking and logic that went into its selection. That "favored" capability stood as the official one of the headquarters of issue. Each headquarters thus reached its own decision, even though intelligence information on which the decision was based might be the same as that considered by others.*

These formal, written G-2 estimates were issued at irregular intervals, but were always issued prior to an operation and during operations as prompted by changes in the enemy situation or changes in the commander's mission. For Sicily, the Seventh Army published six, three before the invasion and three more during the campaign. For its campaigns in Europe in 1944 and 1945, the Third Army published fourteen. In the Third Army, normal distribution required some 150 copies.

Other intelligence reports were distributed within the command as they were required to keep staff members informed. In Patton's commands, these reports consisted chiefly of bulletins and target area analyses. The target area analyses contained data necessary for direct application to operational planning, usually prepared jointly by the G-2 and engineer sections or extracted from studies prepared by higher headquarters. They included such a variety of subjects as beach studies, enemy railroad situations, the feasibility of mounting seaborne operations, river crossings, and the Siegfried Line. In all, twenty-eight such analyses were issued by the Third Army in Europe.

The intelligence bulletins reported on items of current interest and were designed to provide intelligence officers with background material directly or indirectly connected with their business of knowing the enemy. The Third Army in Europe issued sixty such bulletins covering 224 items. Among the subjects covered were prevailing conditions inside Germany, effects on Germany of the loss of the Ruhr, data on German rocket production, the defenses of Berlin, the Remagen Rhine crossing, the National Redoubt, the status of the German Officers' Corps, and the Hitler Youth. As a matter of routine, these bulletins were confined to four mimeographed pages or less in length.

It was not through the written report alone that the intelligence picture was drawn, however. Through oral briefings, complicated military stories could be quite simply told. Two such briefings were held daily in Patton's headquarters. The first, normally taking place at 8:00 A.M., was a special briefing attended by Patton, key members of his staff, the commanding general of the supporting Tactical Air Command unit and his chief of staff, and, as appropriate, distinguished guests and visitors.

---

* The Alpine Redoubt was a notable example. The Third Army, using the same intelligence available to all higher commands, was the only one to correctly write the Redoubt off as a myth.

These briefings were usually quite informal. The standard procedure was for me, using a portable map or blackboard posted specifically for the purpose, to present a resumé of enemy activities of the previous day and enemy capabilities as they appeared to me at the moment. My presentation would be followed by a period of "thinking out loud" by all present. All told, the sessions rarely lasted beyond fifteen minutes.

"If the enemy does so and so," General Patton would ask, "what do you think of our doing this?"

A member of his staff would probably remark that "if such and such does happen we are in a position to do this...."

General Patton then might say, "I'm going to do this—or this—depending upon the situation at that time." Or, "I'm going to suggest this to Bradley or Ike."

Then, turning to General Weyland, the TAC commander, he would ask, "How about it, 'Opey'? Can you give us air support?"

General Weyland's reply was always the same, always in the affirmative. Still better, his frequent answer was, "I've already laid that on," or "We're doing that today."

This early-hour briefing led to a most fruitful exchange of ideas. But of even greater importance, it made everyone there aware of what the commander had in mind, what he would do under various circumstances that might arise. The staff was kept up to date with Patton's thinking on a daily basis. Future plans were laid and made known and an intimacy of thinking developed. At the same time, many items were covered whose relative importance would not justify calling a special staff conference during the day.

The results of these discussions would be transmitted by those present to others who were not in attendance but whose activities were involved or affected.

This early, informal session, held in a small tent, a staff office, or in the open as circumstances dictated, was promptly followed by a formal briefing session in the war room. The war room was a superbly done briefing area, completely furnished with maps and other briefing aids. Electrically lighted by field generators with German helmets forming lampshades above the maps, it provided an appropriate and functional setting.

Those attending the freewheeling, free-thinking earlier briefing normally moved en masse to the war room, there to participate by presence only. Except for official announcements or items upon which Patton might specifically wish them to comment, they had little to say.

A G-2 Section staff officer would start the regular briefings by presenting the enemy situation. He would be followed by a member of the G-3 Section with the friendly situation, then a report on accomplishments of the Tactical Air Command. All would use up-to-the-minute maps and charts. The public relations officer would close with news of events at home, and the situation in other theaters or around the world as reported by the press. On occasion, these regular subjects would be followed by special items presented by other staff members. The total time alloted for the briefing was about twenty minutes.

G-1 Section data such as casualty and replacement figures were kept posted and readily visible. So were any G-4 Section items of general interest, tonnages and the gasoline supply situation, for example. No intelligence estimates were given at this time but, if appropriate, short discourses would be given on such subjects as particular enemy defenses or river crossings. Terrain studies, weather forecasts, enemy personnel and materiel losses and similar data were presented in graphic form and remained in the room for more leisurely and detailed analysis by those directly concerned. A total of about forty persons, including all general and special staff section chiefs and all G-2 subsection chiefs, normally attended the formal briefings.

The G-3 Section's chief liaison officer was always among those present, as was the public relations officer. The former thus was prepared to brief other liaison officers with the command upon their daily call, while the public relations officer was prepared to brief the press. Press briefings were normally given twice a day, morning and night, supplemented on occasion by specially scheduled briefings from General Patton personally.

Like the war room in which they were conducted, the formal briefings were entirely functional. There was no window dressing. In Patton's commands, everyone knew what was going on every day. The briefings served their purpose well.

13

GEORGE SMITH PATTON, JR.

The military reputation of George Smith Patton, Jr., had been well established with his contemporaries long before he gained national and international public recognition in World War II. As a young cavalry officer he had represented the United States in pentathalon competition in the Olympic Games in Stockholm in 1912. Hard on the heels of that he attended the French Cavalry School at Saumur, there to learn and bring back to the United States the arts and techniques of horsemanship and horsemastership. In World War I he gained a lasting reputation as a pioneer tanker in combat and, combining valor and meritorious service in positions of great responsibility, won the Distinguished Service Cross, the Distinguished Service Medal, the Silver Star, and the Purple Heart.

But many a junior cavalry officer, then recently commissioned in the Regular Army under the provisions of the National Defense Act of 1920, would first become acquainted with the name of Patton in another way—through their familiarity with the Patton Saber. A Master of the Sword, Patton had designed this particular weapon, which they carried as standard equipment. Had the young officer of that day been sufficiently observant he might have noted in this saber the characteristics of its designer. A straight-to-the-point, double-edge blade which had replaced a Civil War vintage model of the type wielded and parried, it was designed to strike the enemy head-on, driven home at full speed by the horseman—a weapon of thrust.

Patton was an avid student with a remarkable memory (his fifth year of studies at the United States Military Academy notwithstanding). His interests fell in many directions. He was a polo player of note who trained his own horses, and an ocean navigator, one day to pilot his own yacht with his family aboard to what was then a little-known speck in the far reaches of the Pacific, Hawaii. He also piloted his own aircraft.

The Patton family was a close-knit unit. Patton and his wife, Beatrice, shared many common interests with their children, their daughters Beatrice and Ruth Ellen and their son George S. III. When the children were home from their schools it was not unusual to see the entire family riding together in the hunt or in horse shows, either as individuals in various classes or in pairs. All were somewhat retiring in nature, but all enjoyed social events to the extreme. It was a deeply religious family. Writing and poetry seemed to come naturally to the individual family members.

Patton had chosen the cavalry as his basic branch of service upon leaving the Military Academy in 1909. Graduated from the Mounted Service School in 1914, he stayed on for the cherished second-year course, a highly selective class to which many cavalrymen aspired but to which relatively few were assigned. In World War I he was assigned to Europe with General John J. Pershing's headquarters as a major. It was there that he met his next love in combat—the tank corps, new and highly mobile. Patton became a lieutenant colonel in March of 1918, then a colonel in October of that same year. According to the custom of the service in that era, he was discharged from his temporary rank in June of 1920, to revert to his permanent status of major of the cavalry.

George Patton loved the military life. He was by nature a leader of men, destined to be accepted as one of the country's great military minds. But he never ceased to study the military sciences. His upward advance in the Army was not by chance; it resulted from hard work and avid preparation and application. He was graduated from the Cavalry School advanced course at Fort Riley, Kansas, in 1923, to continue on at the Command and General Staff School at Fort Leavenworth, Kansas, where he was recognized as an honor graduate in the class of 1924. He was later graduated from the Army War College. He received his first star, as brigadier general, in 1940, and was promoted to major general before the Moroccan invasion. His third star, as lieutenant general, followed in Tunisia and his fourth, indicating his rank as full general, was received in Europe.

In pre-war days, as commander of the 2nd Armored Division, Patton had attracted wide attention. Part of planned training maneuvers in Louisiana once had to be canceled when Patton's force captured the "enemy" force by tactics other commanders would have considered impossible. The future would bear out those who predicted then that George Patton was headed for bigger and better things. In Europe alone in World War II he would, at one time or another, have under his command six different army corps and forty-two divisions, twenty-six of them infantry, fourteen armored, and two airborne.

It would be Patton whom the Allies called upon to take command when the situation was bleak and uninviting: in Tunisia after the Kasserine Pass debacle, into the Ardennes to stem the tide of the German breakthrough in the Battle of the Bulge. It also would be Patton who would be deflected southward into Bavaria near the war's end to face Hitler's rumored Redoubt in the fastnesses of the Alps. And it would be Patton whose Third Army fought in four directions after emerging from the Cherbourg Peninsula—only to be set down to wait for gasoline and ammunition and tires and the impedimenta of war at a time when the fortresses of Metz were within his grasp, to be withdrawn to do it again another day when the enemy was set to receive his assaults. His accomplishments in moving men and supplies as the Third Army rolled across Europe would become one of the legends of World War II.

It was during his pre-war command of the 2nd Armored that Patton gained the nickname which was to become a permanent attachment, "Old Blood and Guts." At one of the early regular weekly conferences attended by all the officers of the division, he closed his discussion of some administrative matters with, "And now I will get to my favorite subject: blood and guts."

From that time on it was not uncommon on days of the weekly officers' call to hear someone say, "Let's go over and hear 'Old Blood and Guts.'" The division officers looked forward to these sessions without fear of boredom; Patton never let them down.

With the American entry into the war, Patton was reassigned from the 2nd Armored Division to the planning for the invasion of French Morocco, by way of the Desert Training Center in southern California. Having been alerted to his assignment to take command of the Africa-destined Western Task Force, he stopped by at Fort Bragg, North Carolina, to visit his old division. As in older days, a division assembly was held and there he hinted of his selection for an important assignment elsewhere. He then told how he had been called into the office of General George C. Marshall, Army chief of staff, and informed of that assignment. As he thanked General Marshall for giving him such an opportunity, he related, General Marshall said words to the effect that, "I had nothing to do with your selection; 2nd Armored Division selected you."

Telling the story, however, proved too much for Patton. His gratitude and emotions got the best of him and he choked up, cutting short his talk to the division.

General Harmon, who had by this time taken over command of the division, remarked on the incident later in the day, after Patton's departure. "The damned old fool," Harmon said, with all due reverence. "All the way out here he was telling me about how he was going to raise hell with the troops and so on, and instead of that he broke down and cried!"

With the invasion of French Morocco and the subsequent action in North Africa, Patton rapidly gained a reputation as one of the Allies' most able and most colorful commanders. He had anticipated with some relish the coming clash with the crafty Rommel, yet maintained a calm which seemed remarkable even to the members of his staff. Moving into the initial phase of attack, he advanced II Corps headquarters to Feriana at a time when that area was actually in front of one of his divisions in "no man's land." He could usually be found at the front, but after returning to headquarters at night to await late reports, he would often be seen sitting calmly and reading a book which was totally unrelated to the military. (His staff members were to become accustomed to this, one of them recalling vividly a later scene in Sicily in which everyone else in the area of the command post was hugging the ground to avoid fragmentation from enemy shelling while General Patton sat quietly reading in his camp chair, apparently oblivious to what was happening around him.)

*****

While those who had served under Patton previously were quite aware of his penchant for stern discipline, troops of the II Corps in Tunisia required some indoctrination. They received it, and in short order. A particular concern of their commander was the wearing of the helmet, or "tin hat" as it was commonly called by the troops. The helmet, Patton often commented, was given to the individual soldier not to inconvenience him but to protect him. He insisted that it be worn at all times. The helmet came to be known in the Patton commands as "the twenty-five dollar derby" because the offender caught without one was subject to a twenty-five dollar fine.

After an aide was killed in Tunisia when an artillery shell concussion caused his helmet to snap his head back and break his neck, however, General Patton issued standing orders that the helmet chin strap never be worn under the chin by anyone in his command.

General Patton insisted that all uniform regulations be obeyed.

"Soldiers are always contrary," he once remarked. "I'd issue them coats without buttons, and I'll bet that within twenty-four hours they'd find some, sew them on, and keep them buttoned."

One cold and rainy evening in North Africa he spotted two troopers walking toward a mess hall, one of them wearing a raincoat draped over his shoulders and flapping in the wind.

"Sergeant, come here," the general called.

Moving closer and saluting, the soldier replied, "Sir, I am a warrant officer."

"That simplifies it," General Patton snapped. "You are fined twenty-five dollars." (Under the *Manual of Courts-Martial* he could personally fine an officer or warrant officer, while an enlisted man would have had to be tried.)

News of such actions spread rapidly and had an electrifying effect on Patton's troops. While many complained loudly at the time—exercising the soldier's universally recognized prerogative—the overall effect was splendid, and in the long run had much to do with the pride and spirit evident among the men of Patton's commands.

But it was not discipline alone which created the spirit which permeated Patton's troops, from top staff officers downward. He was a commander who earned the respect of his men, a firm adherent to the philosophy that it was a commander's duty to lead his men, not push them. In the field he was demanding along almost any line—but always with objectives in mind. He held the profession of arms almost as a matter of knighthood: chivalrous, gentlemanly, heroic, never to be downgraded under any circumstances. It was an honor to die, if need be, for one's country. But it wasn't necessary to die to become a hero.

Patton had great sympathy for prisoners of war. To him, being taken prisoner was invariably the fault of the commander, not the prisoner; command had failed, not the man. These feelings, too, were evidenced early, on an occasion at the Cavalry School when he was executive of the academic division in the mid-1930s. When an instructor referred to "PW cages," the term then in the books on prisoner of war handling, Patton interrupted. The term "cage" connoted animals, Patton said. Prisoners of war were men, and generally were not there of their own volition. Henceforth, reference would be to PW "enclosures," not cages. And so it was.

Military courtesy, as appropriate, would be extended by Patton to the enemy as well. In the early days of fighting in Brittany a German general was among those captured by troops of the Third Army. General Patton saw him personally in his van. As one professional soldier to another, he told the German, he was sorry to have to take him prisoner. The enemy officer was assured that he would receive the treatment to which his rank entitled him.

The same attitude prevailed at Metz when a German colonel was captured. Patton invited him into his office, offered him a chair and cigar, and chatted with him about the profession of arms. Such cordial treatment was totally lacking, however, when next a local Nazi political chieftain appeared, slovenly in uniform and distinctly lacking in military bearing. Patton ordered him to stand at attention and speak only when told to speak.

*****

Once criticized for not surrounding himself with brilliant staff officers, General Patton said he preferred loyal ones. When he issued a directive to a member of his staff, he seldom interfered with the way that directive was carried out. He was proud of his official family and made no attempt to hide it. On those occasions when dignitaries visited his headquarters he frequently called in his staff officers to meet them, asking pertinent questions and nodding his head in approval as staff members presented ideas. On one occasion in France, when particularly proud of the achievements of his subordinates, Patton remarked, "You know, Julius Caesar would have a tough time being a brigadier general in this army!"

In June, 1943, during planning for the invasion of Sicily, an important briefing was held for the higher command, up to and including the Allied Force headquarters. A number of top dignitaries, both American and British, were present. A tight time schedule had been worked out. Some thirty minutes were allowed for presentation of the complete operation plan of Patton's Force 343 (later the Seventh Army). The staff presentation was excellent, finished well within the time allotted. The same, unfortunately, could not be said of all the presentations that day. In the break which followed the Force 343 portion of the briefing, General Patton came to each of his participating staff officers, shook his hand, and thanked him for the splendid work. If this were the kind of act which might be interpreted by others as showmanship, it certainly was not considered such by the recipients of their commander's regards.

Toward war's end, the G-3, G-4, and artillery, engineer, and medical section chiefs of the Third Army had all attained general officer rank. Patton never could understand why some of his staff officers were promoted to general and others—whom he periodically and recurrently recommended—were not. All were equally important to him, certainly not subordinate to one another. He went to great lengths in his attempts to correct the situation. One day, in the temporary absence of his two European superiors, Bradley and Eisenhower, he sent forward a letter to the War Department once again making recommendations for these promotions, initiating it and signing it as Third Army commander. Then, he added favorable endorsements as the acting Army Group commander and for the Supreme Allied Commander, again over his personal signatures. To these he added a personal, handwritten note to the Secretary of War in Washington, whom he knew well. This, he thought, would surely bring results. But again, much to his consternation, the promotions were not forthcoming.

Patton used his staff to full advantage at all times. He had a remarkable grasp of what was going on within it. He was never burdened with details unless he needed them, but his operational staff was always close at hand and available, consulted when necessary—and never ignored. Staff members knew it was not necessary to get his prior approval before taking such action as they felt necessary in performance of their duties when these duties were in line with established policies. He expected this of them. There was always a staff buoyancy in this feeling of confidence that their commander was behind them. The overall result was a staff which was integrated completely. There were no jealousies, petty or otherwise. All belonged to the Patton team, and were playing members.

*****

Many times the question has been asked whether Patton possessed an intuition—a sixth sense or whatever—which contributed to the exploits of his commands and to his ability to catch his enemy unaware. If one can call anticipation of enemy reactions based on a lifetime of professional training and on thinking and application "intuition," he had it. He was a professional soldier, a student of history, a planner all his life, beginning in boyhood. He was a general officer long before stars adorned his shoulders. Anything he had done that would have military application later was stored in his retentive memory, to be applied at the first opportunity. He was a military analyst, always analyzing what the result would be if certain other things happened first. If it were possible, he would be the one to make those other things happen.

A firm believer in the cavalry motto, *mobilitate Vigemus*—"In mobility lies our strength"—Patton was a master of the old horse cavalry tactic of the breakthrough, its exploitation, and pursuit. His principles were not unique, but his applications were. He figured enemy reactions in simple formulae, applying the tactical concept that it would take a certain minimum of time for a large enemy force to react. By progressively following up his first action by a second in less than that minimum, he would catch his enemy in the act of maneuvering to react to the first, and so on, *ad infinitum*. This would continue as long as the situation was in his control.

Keeping the enemy off balance by such relentless pursuit was sometimes extremely hard on his own troops, but harder, Patton would point out, on the enemy. The pursuer can stop; the pursued cannot. "We may be tired," he would say, "but think of the enemy. They're the ones doing the running." He would keep up the pressure until the enemy was caught and pinned down, meanwhile maneuvering around the flank to the enemy's rear if possible—again, one of the basic tactics of the cavalry. Patton executed it with vigor.

The mind, too, must be kept mobile, Patton said. One must be able to adjust to changing conditions without stopping things to make that mental adjustment. In planning, he insisted, the situation must be considered mobile, since a mobile situation would be the most difficult. Anything which would work in a mobile situation without further refinement would work in a static one, while the reverse was not necessarily true.

Patton was aware, of course, that his applications of accepted military principles often did not fit the prescribed method. Academically, crossing columns in troop movement as he did in the Battle of the Bulge would have been considered tactical suicide. "I'd hate to go to Leavenworth (Command and General Staff School) after the war," he remarked in discussing the success of that move. "They'll be giving Us (failing grades) for our successful operations. They're going to be in a tough spot, though, with their tactical principles subject to too many historical exceptions."

One of Patton's most distinctive personal traits was the succinctness of his speech. As a division commander in pre-war days, he sent, one day, for both his operations officer and inspector general. Looking up briefly from the paperwork on his desk, he told them, "I want you two to know that I do not judge the efficiency of an officer by the calluses on his butt." Dismissed after that single remark of lightly-disguised advice, the two made haste for the field and began staff inspections, abandoning their desks to their juniors.

Patton had no great love for the British, particularly Montgomery. At Palermo, during the Sicilian campaign, Montgomery paid a courtesy call at Seventh Army headquarters. During the course of the visit, Patton sent for me. In the war room, using maps and relief models, I summarized briefly the enemy situation as seen by the intelligence staff. At the conclusion of the briefing, Montgomery expressed complete agreement with the estimate I'd made. A few hours later, Patton again sent for me.

"I want you to know," he said approvingly, "that you are the only one in this headquarters with whom General Montgomery agrees."

The Patton wit often came to light in press conferences. He kept the press well briefed, at times giving out classified "but not for publication" information as background material on events that were about to unfold. Members of the press, in turn, justified his trust by accepting such information as it was given—in strict confidence. As Patton's forces moved toward the Rhine, the general was asked his opinion of the Siegfried Line—the supposedly impregnable fortification designed to protect the German *Reich* from invasion from the west. "It's a monument to stupidity," he responded without hesitation.

The Siegfried Line, Patton explained, was manmade. And in an age when such natural obstacles as the Alps and the oceans were no longer a matter of concern, anything man had made man could overcome. After all, he added, the German fortification really was nothing more than a line of concrete teeth set in the ground along the bank of a river!

Patton was a favorite of the press corps for more reasons than one. He filled the gap with news when good news was necessary for the morale of troops and the folks back home. Wherever Patton was, things happened. Correspondents knew it, and they followed Patton when they could. This did not always work in the fiery general's favor, of course. When he slapped soldiers' faces in Sicily, that was news, too. And it was his remarks at a press conference after the end of the war that cost him the command of the Third Army.

If Patton made things exciting for members of the press, on at least one occasion a member of the press reversed that situation. When American and Russian forces met at Linz, the Americans hosted a ceremony immediately after the cessation of hostilities in which Russian commanders and staff were decorated. Later, Patton's headquarters staff was invited by the Russians to be their guests at Oed, across the Danube. It was a gala affair, complete with a visit to one of the castles of Franz Josef (still occupied by ex-royalty), a fly-by of Russian aircraft, decorations for the American officers, a powder room providing real face powder for the guests, a dinner of stuffed pig and caviar—followed by numerous toasts to the great figures of both nations—and a Russian ballet company as the main entertainment.

A woman seen arriving at the Linz airfield at the same time as the Americans strolled over to the column of Russian vehicles waiting to go to the affair. She was assumed by the Americans to be a guest of the Russians. The Russians, in turn, assumed she was a guest of the Americans. She was, in fact, Doris Duke Cromwell, representing an American news service.

As the dinner wore on—it lasted about four hours—the Russian host proposed that the American lady be honored too, as a representative and symbol of American womanhood. This done, General Patton in turn produced an American decoration (provided on the spot by his deputy chief of staff) and honored Russian womanhood by decorating the Moscow Ballet's prima ballerina.

*****

Patton had no patience with those lacking the will to do. As a commander, his own sense of duty was always a worthy example. He expected others to have that same sense to the same degree; he accepted nothing less. He wanted action. A good plan placed in operation today, he insisted, was better than a perfect one to be used next week. He once related an incident from his days at the Military Academy which had greatly impressed him. One day on the football practice field, he wasn't as active as one member of the coaching staff thought he should be. "Mr. Patton," the coach yelled, "what are you standing there for? Do something. Do anything. If you can't do anything else, throw a fit—but do *something!*"

After the Battle of the Bulge, plans were being laid in Third Army headquarters to continue the attack to the east. One of the corps had been advised of the plans which were under way and directed to prepare its own plans accordingly. A briefing was held on a Friday, at which the Third Army staff presentation was followed by a presentation of the corps plan. General Patton, as usual, was sitting in the front row listening attentively. The corps plan was well done and was considered proper.

"When can you attack?" Patton asked.

"Wednesday," was the corps commander's prompt reply.

"That's too late."

The corps commander argued that in view of the weather, which was miserable, and the swollen streams, which were flooding the valleys and flats, Wednesday was the best he could do. Patton said again, "That's too late."

The corps commander presented his case in greater detail. He had rebuilt one road three times in the last twenty-four hours just to keep his vehicles from bogging down completely. Bringing up ammunition was a major problem. But Patton again said Wednesday was too late, and the corps commander rejoined with, "But general, you must remember that it takes time to do these things."

"Then what the hell are you wasting your time here for?" Patton snapped. Monday, he said, would be the day of the corps attack. The conference was over. The corps initiated its attack on Monday night.

General Patton already had this particular corps commander tabbed as a "worrier." Earlier in the Third Army campaign, his corps had been assigned the southern flank on the Third Army plunge across France. That flank rested on the Loire River and was protected only by scattered units, placed at strategic points. In the corps commander's view, the Germans, wedged between the Third Army on their north and the Seventh Army coming up from the Rhone valley, created a threat to the southern flank. Patton did not share that view.

The general received a call in the dark of night from the corps commander, who complained that the flank was insecure. Patton reminded him that back in the academic days at Fort Leavenworth the approved measure was to protect the army's flank by a squadron of horse cavalry, less Troop A. "And you've got a damned sight more than that," the general continued.

The corps continued with its "exposed" southern flank without incident. It was a situation like this which once caused Patton to observe that in war nothing is ever as bad or as good as it is reported to higher headquarters.

*****

Patton expected soldiers, wherever they were, to remember they were Americans and take pride in the uniform they wore. Invited to Nuremberg after the war to present medals and awards at the "Little Olympics" of the military service, he stopped several times in the stadium to reprove soldiers for improper uniform. Reminded by one of the hosts that he was out of the Third Army area and that these troops were not part of his command, Patton replied, "They all have to catch hell once in a while anyway." The soldiers took it in stride.

Patton commanded great respect, from friend and foe alike. Enemy commanders would surrender only to General Patton in person. To be taken by a great field commander apparently added a certain dignity to an otherwise ignominious situation. His presence in other theaters would be regarded by the enemy as a foreboding of things to come. Where Patton was and what he was doing was of constant interest to the enemy high command. He was, as they would say later, a "doer."

A great part of the Patton military genius was his ability to get the best and the most from his men. This he always expected, without compromise. Infantry troops could attack continuously for sixty hours, he said, but after that they must have relief; otherwise, fatigue and loss of sleep would negate their efforts. He realized, on the other hand, that the efficacy of a division attack could be judged in the first four hours.

Patton believed a commander should be seen by his troops. In pre-war maneuvers this meant standing in the dust as his tanks rumbled by, arms extended and hands clasped in the fashion of a victorious prizefighter, and yelling encouragement: "Give 'em hell!" In combat, when the going was tough, it meant visiting the front, getting shot at. He felt it was a great morale builder for the troops to see a commander sharing the danger of his soldiers. The more senior an officer, he contended, the more time he had for visiting the front. He insisted that principal staff officers visit the front, too; he didn't want any "armchair" soldiers.

From Patton, praise came as easily as criticism, and both were voiced only when deserved. He acknowledged his own errors promptly; mistakes made once would not be repeated. His loyalties to his staff and junior officers and his faith in the performance of his command were a constant source of wonderment to the uninitiated.

"Never take counsel of your fears," was standard Patton advice. Cemeteries, he said, should never be placed where they could be seen by replacements moving to the front.

Of all Patton's superiors, it was perhaps Field Marshal Alexander who characterized him best. Lord Alexander, in his memoirs, suggested that Patton should have lived in the Napoleonic era—he would have made a fine marshal for Napoleon.

Whatever else George S. Patton, Jr., did that made history, one thing he left to posterity is the great pride of many ex-soldiers who, even today, when asked what outfit they were in rarely mention regiment, division, corps, or army. Instead, they reply with warm and glowing pride, even if they were among those "bawled out," in a simple statement still understood by an older generation, "I was with Patton."

EPILOGUE:
COMMAND SUPPORT

What the intelligence officer needs most to help him through his day-to-day chores is command support: the support of his commander, evidenced primarily by mutual confidence engendered by and nurtured through respect. He must be confident that the results of his efforts will be respected by his commander, both in terms of interest and attitude and in the degree of utilization of the end product so painstakingly produced. The commander, on the other hand, must be confident that his intelligence chief's work merits such respect. If either's confidence fails, command support is nonexistent. With command support, G-2 will tackle any job. Without it, he performs a purposeless task, merely going through a series of staff exercises. In that case, both he and the commander are losers.

In Patton's commands, intelligence was always viewed as big business and treated accordingly. Although working, by necessity, in the shadows, it always had its place in the sun. It was never viewed as subordinate to any other staff activity. G-2 was never the forgotten man. On many occasions the commander's group included but two others, one of them G-2.

General Patton appreciated the fact that collection of intelligence took time. He knew it took time for reports to filter back, particularly through enemy territory. He knew intelligence had to pierce a wall of fire, that agents on the ground could see only what was within their vision. He knew that they could only report what they had seen or heard under extremely hazardous conditions. He understood that intelligence was not a series of guesses and that unit identifications were particularly difficult to get. (He knew, for example, that the Seventh Army's own troop lists carried almost 250 separate numerically designated Army units which varied in strength from a postal unit of seven men to an anti-aircraft brigade totaling well over 6,000, in addition to his major commands—the corps and divisions, all with different vehicle bumper markings and insignia.) He knew that intelligence was not a matter of crystal gazing and that no occult powers could be called upon to give the answers. He knew that there was nothing mysterious about it, nothing but conscientious application and hard work.

Contrast the command support enjoyed by Patton's intelligence staff with that given the intelligence chief of the Italian Command headquarters, Sixth Army, Armed Forces of Sicily. His *Intelligence Bulletin No. 2*, issued at 5:00 P.M. on July 1, 1943, and captured in the Enna area a few weeks later, reflected a highly skilled intelligence job:

"...The mass of forces and materials of the Anglo-Americans disposed in the Mediterranean—sixty percent of the aviation, ninety percent of the troops, ninety-six percent of the landing equipment—are located in the eastern basin, thus in the sector which directly concerns Sicily....The unanimity of the voicing of the foreign press of both belligerent and neutral countries and information received from good sources, all confirm indications of what the Anglo-Saxons are preparing to undertake.

"...Preparation for such an invasion is now...complete....The period from the first to the tenth of July is especially favorable to the successful approach of enemy vessels on our coast because of the moonless nights....The enemy cannot afford to wait....We must be ready for the start of this operation at any moment....Sicily and/or Sardinia are the enemy objectives. The major probability is an attack on Sicily.

"...It would be a great error to believe that the enemy would undertake a secondary attack. For political and moral reasons of exceptional value, the Anglo-Americans will have to attack with all the strength they have....It is understood that a surprise attack will be undertaken....Keep strict guard everywhere. Halt enemy action during the crises; while the parachutists are dropping and while the landing barges are on the beaches."

How right he was! Sicily was the Allied objective. July 10 was D-Day.

Whatever happened to that Italian intelligence officer is a matter of conjecture. Certainly if he had had the confidence of his commander, some sort of special troop alert should have been forthcoming. His reasoning was good. But the Sicilian command was taken by complete surprise. Though he may well have told his superiors ten days later, "I told you so," that intelligence officer had gone through a staff exercise; for all practical purposes his efforts had been in vain. His air reconnaissances, his photo reconnaissances, the work of his agents, his infiltrations by submarine, and his lone fishing craft surreptitiously plying the waters along the coast of North Africa all proved to be wasted motions.

Whatever else he had, he lacked one thing: the confidence of his commander. He lacked command support.

The commander's group was standing in a grove on high ground just above the invasion beaches in southern Sicily, a few miles east of Gela

General Patton's question was directed to his G-2.

"If I attack Agrigento, will I bring on a major engagement?"

"No, Sir."

Patton looked at G-3, nodding assent.

"Issue the order. "

GLOSSARY

AFHQ—Allied Force Headquarters
Blackstone—North Africa invasion sub-task force
CIC—Counterintelligence Corps
D-Day—debarkation (invasion landing) day
DOL—Detached Officers List
EEI—Essential Element of Information
FFI—French Forces of the Interior
Force 141—code name for Field Marshal Sir Harold Alexander's planning group, Sicilian invasion
Force 163—code name for Seventh U.S. Army planning group, southern France invasion
Force 343—code name for I Armored Corps planning group, Sicilian invasion
Force 545—code name for Field Marshal Sir Bernard L. Montgomery's planning group, Sicilian invasion
G-1—chief officer, personnel section, higher echelons
G-2—chief intelligence officer, higher echelons
G-3—chief operations officer, higher echelons
G-4—chief logistics officer, higher echelons
GLO—ground liaison officer
Ia—operations officer, German Army
Ic—intelligence officer, German Army
ISUM—intelligence summary report
MP—Military Police
Operation Anvil—Allied Mediterranean invasion of southern France
Operation Husky—Allied invasion of Sicily
Operation Overlord—Allied cross-channel invasion of Europe
Operation Skorzeny—clandestine German operation in advance of Ardennes counteroffensive
Operation Torch—Allied invasion of North Africa
OSS—Office of Strategic Services
PW—prisoner of war
ROTC—Reserve Officers Training Corps
S-2—intelligence officer, lower echelon
SHAFE—Supreme Headquarters Allied Expeditionary Force
SIAM—Signal Intelligence and Monitoring
SS—German *Schutzstaffel*, Hitler's elite guard
TAC—Tactical Air Command
Vulture—code name for German Operation Skorzeny
Wacht am Rhein—Operation Watch on the Rhine, German Ardennes counteroffensive

INDEX

A

Afrika Korps 28, 30-31, 33
Agrigento 19, 20, 55, 57, 159
Alexander, British General Sir Harold 31, 34, 38, 68, 156, 160
Algeria 46
Allen, Colonel Robert S. 6, 10, 114, 118, 126-131
Alpine Redoubt 118, 142
Anderson, Major General Johnathan 20, 21
Anfa Conference 38
Anvil 67, 160
Avranches Gap 77

B

Battle of the Bulge 7, 8, 9, 87, 103, 111-114, 137, 141, 147, 152, 154
Blackstone 11, 21, 23, 25, 134, 160
"born at sea, baptized in blood" 53
Bradley, General Omar N. 7, 17, 37, 73, 77, 88, 107, 110, 112, 120, 143, 150

C

Caltanissetta 45, 47
Casablanca 21, 25, 38, 68
Catania Plain 45, 50
Central Task Force 20
Cherbourg Peninsula 69, 73, 147
Churchill, Prime Minister Winston 38
CIC 29, 72, 134, 160
Clark, Lieutenant General Mark W. 28
Corsica 43, 66
Croix de Guerre 30

D

Dickson, Colonel B.A. 31, 36
Dietrich, Colonel General Sepp 91, 96

E

Eastern Task Force 20
EEI 69, 70, 71, 82, 133, 137, 160
Eisenhower, General Dwight D. 7, 9, 112-114, 131, 150
El Guettar 35-37

F

FFI 83, 160
Fifth Army 28, 30, 66
Fort Benning 22
Fort Bragg 20, 25, 147
Fort Leavenworth 16, 127, 146, 155
French Morocco 11, 24, 26, 29-30, 37, 38, 134, 141, 147, 148

G

G-3 17, 19, 99, 135, 138, 143-144, 150, 159, 160
Gabes 34, 35
Gay, Brigadier General Hobart R. "Hap' 38, 78, 115-117
Gela 19, 53-55, 57, 58, 159
Göring, Herman 53, 61

H

Hadjeb 35
Harmon, Major General Ernest N. 21, 24, 147, 123-124
Hewitt, Rear Admiral Henry Kent 21, 38
Hitler 7, 24, 33, 59, 76, 77, 79, 87, 89, 96, 100, 111, 112, 114-
115, 118-119, 129, 142, 147, 160

I

I Armored Corps 11, 28, 37-39, 46, 53, 160
ISUM 32, 37, 139, 160

J

Juin, General Alphonse 66

K

Kasserine Pass 30, 35, 38, 147
Keyes, Major General Geoffrey 38, 57
Koch, Oscar W. 3, 6-13, 19, 21, 69

M

Maddox, Colonel 19, 78
Mareth Line 34
Marshall, General George C. 147
McAuliffe, Brigadier General Anthony C. 110
Messina 45, 50, 56-57, 59, 61, 65
Metz 69, 79, 80-83, 87, 88, 147, 150
Monrovia 49, 55
Montgomery, General Sir Bernard L. 19, 34, 38, 78, 88, 95, 152, 160
Mount Etna 45
Mussolini 24, 33, 59

N

Nancy 79, 82, 87-89, 93, 98, 107, 108-109, 113
North Africa 11, 20, 22-23, 25, 28, 33, 37, 44, 47, 48, 58-59, 66-67, 71, 132, 148-149, 159, 160

O

Operation Husky 41, 44, 160
Oran 20, 46
OSS 44, 72, 83, 126, 135, 138, 140, 160

P

Palermo 19, 20, 57, 58, 61, 65-67, 152
Pas-de-Calais 76-77
Patch, Major General Alexander M. 68
Paulus, Field Marshal Friedrich von 33
Pershing, General John J. 11, 146
PW 35, 48, 83-84, 96, 105, 115, 133, 135, 149, 160

R

Rabat 30, 38-39, 44, 46
Rommel, General Field Marshal Erwin 28, 30-31, 34, 148

S

S-2 14, 160
Sardinia 43, 66, 158
SIAM 32, 160
Siegfried Line 79, 87, 88-89, 106-107, 142, 153
Skorzeny, Otto 100-101, 108, 160
St. Vith 102, 108-111
Strong, General Kenneth 113
Sultan 29, 30, 69

T

TAC 37, 73, 79-80, 83, 87, 90, 105-106, 136, 142-143, 160
Trapani 58
Truscott, Jr., Brigadier General Lucian K. 21

V

Vichy 30
Volks Grenadier 91-94, 96, 98, 102

W

Wedemeyer, Brigadier General Albert 50-51, 54
Western Task Force 20, 24, 26, 28, 30-31, 38, 141, 147

Brig. Gen. Oscar W. Koch (*page 2)* was born in 1897 and died May 16, 1970, after a full and varied military career. He served his country from 1915 until his retirement in 1954, beginning as a member of the Light Horse Squadron Association in Milwaukee, Wisconsin, and ending with service in Korea as commander of the 25th Infantry Division. In 1946, General Koch began the first peacetime combat intelligence school in the Army's history. After retiring from the Army he received a grant from the Guggenheim Foundation for his research in military history, and worked two years for the U.S. State Department in Germany and England.

Robert G. Hays (*at right)* is on the journalism faculty at the University of Illinois, where he has won international awards for his teaching and research. He has been a newspaper reporter, public relations writer, and magazine editor. His books include *Country Editor*, *State Science in Illinois*, *Early Stories From the Land*, and *A Race at Bay*.

Notes